FIND YOUR WAY

FIND
your
WAY

Unleash Your Power and Highest Potential

CARLY FIORINA

TYNDALE
MOMENTUM®

The nonfiction imprint of
Tyndale House Publishers, Inc.

Visit Tyndale online at www.tyndale.com.

Visit Tyndale Momentum online at www.tyndalemomentum.com.

TYNDALE, *Tyndale Momentum*, and Tyndale's quill logo are registered trademarks of Tyndale House Publishers, Inc. The Tyndale Momentum logo is a trademark of Tyndale House Publishers, Inc. Tyndale Momentum is the nonfiction imprint of Tyndale House Publishers, Inc., Carol Stream, Illinois.

The Leadership Framework is a registered trademark of Carly Fiorina.

Find Your Way: Unleash Your Power and Highest Potential

Designed by Jennifer Phelps

Published in association with the literary agency of AGI Vigliano Literary LLC, 16 East 77th Street, 3rd Floor, New York, NY 10075.

Scripture quotations are taken from the *Holy Bible*, King James Version.

For information about special discounts for bulk purchases, please contact Tyndale House Publishers at csresponse@tyndale.com, or call 1-800-323-9400.

ISBN 978-1-4964-3569-9

Printed in the United States of America

25   24   23   22   21   20   19
7   6   5   4   3   2   1

Do not desire to fit in.
Desire to oblige yourselves to lead.

GWENDOLYN BROOKS

CONTENTS

FOREWORD

FOR MANY YEARS, what I knew about Carly Fiorina came mostly from reading about her in various business publications, hearing about her in the news, or seeing her in interviews. Still, from this casual and distant observation, my impression of her was that she was smart, tough, bold, controversial, and not afraid of a fight.

Then, one day I was asked to colead an off-site leadership workshop with Carly for a small group of leaders from across the United States—and my impression of her was broadened by real-life experience.

As I had surmised, she was very smart, experienced, straightforward, and resilient. But what came through repeatedly during the few days we worked together was her *humanity*. As we fielded questions, worked through leadership quandaries presented by the attendees, diagnosed problems, and crafted solutions together, I was impressed by her deep sense of empathy. It was not only clear that she understood the difficult issues these leaders were facing, but she also felt for them and was able to connect with them.

What I'm referring to is not just soft-hearted sympathy or "care for the individual." It was more her capacity to truly understand these leaders—and to let them *know* she understood—while also *joining together with them* to find a way forward. Said another way, she put the head together with the heart. She brought real answers and proven principles that helped these leaders see beyond their confusion or their feeling of being stuck—to see what was possible and achievable. Her intelligence, toughness, and candor were in no way incompatible with her empathy. In fact, quite the opposite. Everything worked together to move people forward to where they wanted to go.

When I read *Find Your Way*, I was similarly impressed. In these pages, I found all the same attributes I had observed in Carly in that initial workshop and in subsequent opportunities we've had to work together on other projects and leadership intensives. I saw the same combination of empathy and deep, practical experience in how things work. I saw audacious goal-setting as well as level-headed solutions for "How am I going to make it through the week?" kinds of problems.

As you read, you will feel understood, as if Carly were speaking directly to you. You will know that she has *been there* and identifies with what you are facing. And she will show you not only a way out of your current dilemma, but also a *path forward* toward the desired future reality that you've been wanting to pursue but perhaps haven't known how.

As a psychologist and a leadership consultant, I could not read this book without my own technical mind kicking in. Although Carly doesn't focus on the psychological, neurological, biological, relational, systemic, emotional, social, and mental *science* behind her methods, I can assure you it is all there. As she tells stories and explains principles, I can see behind her advice an operating system grounded in the best science and research on human performance. I could write an entire commentary on each chapter, explaining how if you will do the simple things she suggests, your neurochemistry will change and engage the parts of your brain that have been stalled or not working to full capacity before now. How your interactions with other people will move them from being obstacles to what you're wanting to achieve to being helpful partners—and actually change their ability to perform. How the creative mind that you need to solve problems will finally wake up, and how you will find yourself with capacities you never realized you had. How your own emotional regulation will change, propelling you toward outcomes you haven't seen before. Carly's simple four-step problem-solving model alone will move you forward in unbelievable ways.

But enough about the wonky nerd stuff behind the curtain. As you read this book, what matters is that you will get to experience firsthand the helpful, proven wisdom and deep care that I have seen in working alongside Carly in leadership development.

I will close this brief introduction with perhaps the greatest endorsement I could give. I have two daughters, and I am not what you would call a "controlling" father. I believe in granting them great freedom and autonomy. But in this case, I'm putting my foot down: They *will* read this book.

Dr. Henry Cloud
Los Angeles, California

MOMENT OF REVELATION

A Word on Your One Wild and Precious Life

I WAS A MISERABLE first-year law-school student, suffering yet another massive migraine, standing in the shower in the upstairs bathroom of my parents' house on an otherwise uneventful Sunday morning, when the revelation hit me: *I could just quit.*

Quit?

Surely I had that wrong.

I couldn't *quit.*

My parents were well acquainted with struggle in life, and they were determined that their circumstances would not define them. My mother, the only child of an auto assembly-line worker, had lost her own mother at age ten. She grew up with the proverbial evil stepmother. She was a bright student, a valedictorian, but her father refused to allow her to attend college. So she ran away from home at eighteen and somehow made her way to Texas to join the Women's Army Corps. She eventually became the secretary to the commanding officer at the military base, which is how she met my father.

Mom was a richly talented artist who mostly put her art aside while she poured herself into her three children—determined they would have the education, the experiences, and the opportunities she had not.

My father grew up with a noticeable physical deformity in a tiny Texas town. When he was thirteen, his father and brother died within nine months of each other, and his mother never fully recovered from the shock and grief. After World War II, he went to the "wrong" law school—University of Texas, before anyone had ever heard of it—definitely not Harvard or Yale. He succeeded in law by dint of sheer hard work and intellectual prowess. He eventually became dean of Duke University Law School, a deputy US attorney general, and a federal judge on the Ninth Circuit Court of Appeals. He taught his children that they would succeed if they just kept going when the going got tough.

My parents were not quitters. They were not sympathetic to the phrase "I don't like it." Hard work and perseverance were their credo, and what they wanted more than anything was for me to fulfill my potential. They both thought that following my father's footsteps into the legal profession was the right plan for me.

I knew how much they had invested in me. I knew how many of their hopes and dreams were reflected in me. I knew they had overcome so much more than I could understand.

Surely I couldn't just quit!

Still, I was ready to quit.

Until that point in my life, the only thing I truly excelled at was *people pleasing*, particularly *parent* pleasing. I worked hard to please my parents—much to the resentment of my brother and sister at times.

I was not going to be the one to disappoint Mom and Dad.

However, by the second day of class, I knew I *hated* law school. When my dad came to visit, I told him how much I hated it. I told him about the constant headaches, and the complete lack of joy or interest I felt each time I walked into the classroom.

"Give it a year, Carly," he said. "See how you feel then."

A year sounded like an eternity to me.

Shortly after his visit, I traveled home to see my parents. I did not have in mind that I would quit that weekend. Nevertheless, it was during that trip, while standing in the shower one morning, that I made up my mind. This was my *life . . .* what poet Mary Oliver calls my *"one wild and precious life."*[1] It didn't feel wild or precious just then. It felt dreadful and disappointing at best.

I craved the wild-and-precious thing.

Resolved, I dressed, headed downstairs, ushered my parents together, and plunged headlong into my announcement.

"I hate law school. It is not what I am meant to do. I quit."

My father said the worst thing he could have said: "Carly, I am very disappointed. I am afraid you may not amount to anything . . ."

Ugh.

My mother, looking very grave, asked, "What are you going to do?"

"I don't know."

I don't know? I don't know?! I have always known what came next!

I did not want to disappoint my parents. I felt heartbroken by their obvious resignation to the fact that their daughter was making a terrible, terrible mistake.

And not knowing what came next, I felt terrified.

Still, I did not want to sign up for a life that wasn't my own. I was heartbroken and terrified, but by the end of that agonizing conversation with my parents, I also realized that I felt totally, utterly *free*.

The following day, I flew back to Los Angeles, packed up my sparse belongings, and vowed never, ever to look back.

I spend a fair amount of time these days speaking to civic organizations, university students, corporate audiences, church groups, and others. I love connecting with people from a variety of walks of life in these somewhat intimate forums, and I always stick around after my talks to greet anyone who cares to chat. I've given hundreds of talks, maybe even thousands by now, and after nearly every one, at least one person has approached me to say, "Thank you. I feel so lifted up."

It's uncanny how often this happens, and it's always those same two simple words: *lifted up*.

In a day and age when so many people feel anxious and overwhelmed, hopeless and helpless, weary and annoyed and afraid, such a boost is no small thing. We need our *sights* lifted from our present circumstances to what is possible in the days to come. We need our *thoughts* lifted from negative self-talk and chronic comparisons to confirmation of what makes us distinct. We need our *hearts* lifted from despondency and despair to openness, expansiveness, and peace.

I've come to believe there are two kinds of people, both in your relational sphere and in mine. There are those who push us down, tempting us to tap into the worst, smallest, most self-centered version of ourselves; and there are those who lift us up, compelling us to reach for the best *us* we've ever known.

I've written this book with the singular desire to be the kind of person who lifts you up. My hope is that the lessons I've learned since that moment of revelation in the shower, and the decisions I've made to reclaim my own power, take possession of my own life, and find my own way, will be instructive—and inspiring—for you as well.

I know what it feels like to possess an abundance of anxiety and a scarcity of peace. I know what it's like to try to live someone else's dream, to strive for someone else's goal, and to attempt to get where I'm going by following someone else's plan. I know what that soul-level dissatisfaction feels like. I know the drudgery. I know the disappointment. I know the pain.

But that's not all I know. Along with that decision to take back the power that had been mine all along—the power to assess, the power to reason, the power to *choose*—came a new wave of learning and insight. Among other things, I learned these key principles:

- Fulfillment is found by first tending to our own souls.
- Decisions that are right today are those we can look back on without regret for the rest of our lives.
- The burden of other people's expectations is a weight we can—and should—put down.

There is only one wild and precious life with your name on it, just waiting to be lived. The chapters that follow will show you how.

part one

THE PURPOSE OF THE PATH

chapter one

FUTURE YOU

The Only Limitless
Asset Around

No MATTER WHERE you are in your life right now, and no matter where you've been, you are not yet all you can be. If I were to net out the big idea of this book in one neat line, that's it: *You are not yet all you can be.* Life can shift. Circumstances shift. You can glean fresh understanding. You can change. You can grow. And as you seize the opportunities that are within you and right in front of you, you'll find a certain steadiness in your life that perhaps you've never known before.

You see, though my undergraduate degree in medieval history (yes, I know) didn't exactly point me toward a lucrative career after graduation, it provided me with a gift that has proved invaluable throughout my life: *perspective.* To study history is to be reminded that one thing has remained the same down through the ages. Amid all the changes in culture, technology, and knowledge, the one thing that has stayed the same is *us.*

People.

People *never* change. Sure, we change our hairstyles, fashion trends, home décor, exercise regimens, parenting approaches, spending patterns, modes of transportation, preferred forms of entertainment, culinary

No matter where you are in your life right now, you are not yet all you can be.

tastes, and relationship patterns all the time. But behind and beneath and alongside all that window dressing is the same human soul that has always been there, longing for the same things we've always wanted: *meaning, purpose, fulfillment, dignity, love,* and *peace.*

I started a foundation called Unlocking Potential to provide an opportunity for staff of nonprofits to get better at their work. Many nonprofits are solving—or seeking to solve—some of the most severe and intractable problems in human society; and yet, historically, precious little investment has been made to lift up these people, provide them with the training they need, and celebrate the important contributions they make in communities around the world. Specifically, I wanted every nonprofit we worked with to learn how to magnetize and retain strong leaders who would consistently take personal responsibility, better navigate critical transitions, speak a common language of leadership, and help others in their organizations to grow. When these groups were reminded of the power they already possessed, they felt inspired to thrive. We saw this potential unlocked through our partnerships.

These results are tremendously gratifying to me personally because they validate two of my most fundamental beliefs: (1) Every person possesses astounding God-given potential, and (2) their potential can be unleashed.

Think about it: Human potential is the only limitless resource in the world. Not time. Not money. Not skill. Not fame, beauty, or charm. I don't care if you're jaw-droppingly gorgeous, at the top of your vocational game, or have more money than you know what to do with—at some point, those wells may run dry. Wrinkles will show up, and your vitality will begin to wane. The needs of the marketplace

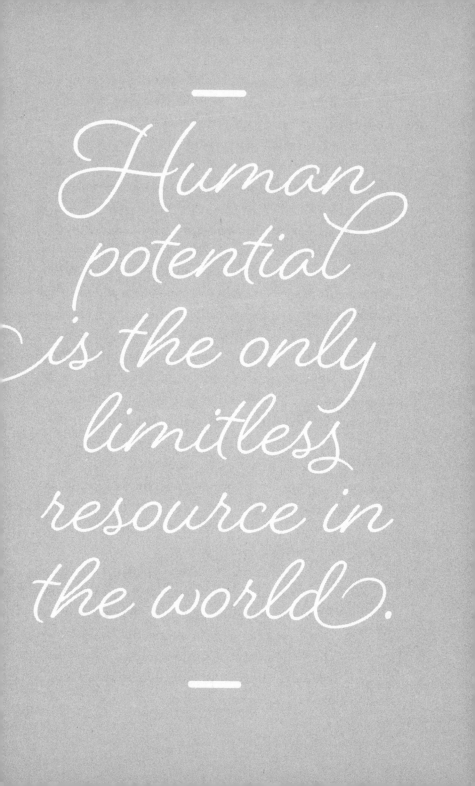

Human potential is the only limitless resource in the world.

may shift. The stock market might plummet, leaving you with an empty or depleted portfolio. But that is never the case with human potential. *Who you might become* is forever before you, beckoning you onward. *What you might accomplish* keeps whispering your name. However much of your potential you unleash, there is always more, just waiting to be tapped into.

You and I have both heard heard stories about children whose potential was recognized early—as a dancer, a chess master, a debater, or a lawyer—and who grew up surrounded by people who helped them realize their potential and live a full and fulfilling life. But for most of us, life isn't like that. I have known people who, even at the end of their lives, felt as if they never found their calling or realized their potential. Perhaps you know some of these people too. My hope is that by the time you reach the end of this book, you will be on the path to unlocking your full potential and reclaiming your own power.

————

If you're like most of the women and men my team and I have worked with, this process of realizing your fullest potential will feel as if something inside you is being unlocked.

Realizing your fullest potential will feel as if something inside you is being unlocked.

We've all had the experience of feeling "locked up." My latest visit to the dentist's chair comes to mind. It must be part of a hygienist's formal training, this knack for asking in-depth questions of their poor patients who sit with water spigots, tiny vacuum cleaners, and a stranger's hands stuck in their mouths.

Can't you tell that we're all locked up down here?

I also think of being wedged into an airplane seat at thirty thousand feet, flying through the middle of a thunderhead. Perhaps nothing has improved my prayer life quite like running for president. Let me tell you, all those cross-country flights on mini-me airplanes that require you to duck your head as you make your way to your seat, lest you crack your skull on the ceiling, force a *deep* faith. When we would hit turbulence, I would reflexively flatten my palm against the window, as if I could single-handedly keep the plane aloft.

Just get this thing on the ground safely, I would silently will the pilot, who was seated only six feet away. *Locked up* is precisely how I felt.

Or what about when you're stuck in bed sick while others are out having fun? I was due to fly to Chicago not long ago for a series of meetings that mattered greatly to me, but on the morning of my departure I awoke with a bad case of laryngitis. When I tried to greet my husband, I sounded about as smooth as a Texas bullfrog. Wanting to verbalize but having no voice? Yes, that's a bit like being locked up.

And then there's *dieting*. If you want to experience a locked-up sensation, give the Whole30 plan a try. No bread. No cheese. No ice cream. No fun. But to the diet creators' credit, at least it's only for thirty days. I have heard of people who eat like cavemen for a *lifetime*, which makes me wonder: Do they sneak doughnuts from the office breakroom when nobody's looking?

Surely a few of them must.

Indeed, the thing that helps us move through these experiences of feeling locked up is just that: *It's only a feeling;*

we're not actually locked up. We know that eventually the dentist appointment will end, the plane will land, the sickness will abate, and we'll eat bread and cheese once again. But what about being *endlessly* locked up? How would we cope with that?

Consider those on death row, or elsewhere in our prison system, with no chance for parole. What does being *locked up* mean to them?

Or those who suffer a life-changing event—a stroke, a traumatic brain injury, a devastating car accident—that forever alters their mobility, their personality, their ability to function. Would they say that they feel locked up? When I went through treatment for breast cancer—the chemo, the hair loss, the ensuing surgeries and infections and pain— I wondered about things like *permanence*. Would I ever feel whole again? And when my husband, Frank, and I lost our younger daughter, Lori Ann, at age thirty-five, only eight months after my devastating cancer diagnosis, it made my darkest days even darker.

Lori Ann knew well the feeling of being locked up. She suffered from addiction. And then, in a moment, her astounding potential was *gone*.

You and I both recognize these two types of being locked up—the temporary and the permanent. And yet there is a third, more tragic, form of paralysis we often overlook—that is, *the locked-up states we choose for ourselves.*

Just off Fisherman's Wharf in San Francisco Bay, between the Golden Gate Bridge and Treasure Island, sits Alcatraz Island, home to the infamous federal prison where, between 1934 and 1963, the most hardened criminals in the country were sent. Chicago Mafia boss Al Capone and violent murderer Robert Stroud, better known as the Birdman of Alcatraz, both did time there. Yet, even within the walls of this notoriously harsh prison, there was a place where even the roughest, toughest prisoners admitted defeat: D Block.

D Block was where the solitary-confinement cell was located, a soul-crushing "time-out" for prisoners who misbehaved.

Known as "the hole," the solitary-confinement cell was a soundproof, six-by-eight-foot space outfitted with only a bed frame, a toilet, and a small sink. General-population prisoners who were viewed as an imminent threat to others, or who violated prison rules, were placed in solitary confinement for up to nineteen consecutive days, during which they had no human contact and no exposure to light, except for the three-times-daily check-ins by a guard. During those meal breaks, the heavy outer door would open, allowing a shaft of light to stream through the room's inner metal bars, and a tray of food, all lumped together, would be slid through a special opening. After about twenty minutes, the tray was returned, and the doors were closed, casting the cell back into pitch darkness.

Still today, if you visit Alcatraz as a tourist, you can opt to experience one of these isolation chambers for a few minutes, along with several others in your tour group. After being ushered into the cell, you are given a quick overview, and then the heavy door is slammed shut. There is nothing quite like the sensation of being in a space so dark and desolate that you can neither hear the outside world nor see your hand directly in front of your face. Whatever good you might bring to the world around you fades to black as you stand there hopeless, helpless, and afraid.

Now imagine choosing this fate not as an hour-long tourist attraction, but as a way of life. Real life. *Your one and only wild and precious life.*

My attempt at law school wasn't the only time I did this to myself. When I was in my twenties, I entered into a marriage unsure of who I was and what I wanted out of life. The man I married was interesting, charming, and more experienced than I was. My mother was suspicious of him from the outset, and she tried to warn me, but she couldn't articulate her concerns in words I was able to hear at the time. So I said "I do" to someone who would betray every one of our vows.

This *locked-up* feeling I'm describing? That's exactly how I felt after just a few years of marriage. In my heart, I know I did everything I could to make our relationship work, but I was unsuccessful. After six and a half years, when the truth about my husband's disloyalty had become plain for me to see, I knew I had to get out of this irretrievably broken relationship. Despite my best efforts and intentions, I found it impossible to stay married to someone who shrugged off commitment and everything good about married life.

I remember standing with him in the kitchen one night, asking him for the umpteenth time to sign the separation agreement my lawyer had drawn up.

I politely asked him to sign.

He refused.

I impolitely asked him to sign.

He refused.

I then *pleaded* with him to sign, rationally enumerating all the reasons that showed our marriage had already died.

Again, he stubbornly refused.

Silently, calmly, I stepped to the cupboard, opened the cabinet door, and removed a single plate from the shelf. I threw the plate at the kitchen floor and stood perfectly still as the china shattered into a thousand pieces. Now that I had his attention, with jagged shards of china all around us, I drew upon the only remaining leverage I had. Yes, I played the mother-in-law card. I looked at the man I had once loved dearly and said with steely determination, "If you do not sign this agreement, I will call my mother. She will come to visit, and she will stay with us, here, under our roof. And she will not leave until you sign these papers."

He signed.

Whether we're talking about an introvert in a sea of type A personalities, a thoroughbred trying to survive in a donkey-paced work environment, an imaginative dreamer tucked inside an accountant, a willing friend who finds herself friendless, a contributor who questions her ability to contribute, or a would-be success story needing assurance that she won't fail, nobody in their right mind stays locked up voluntarily. And yet this is exactly what I see countless people do each day, in every imaginable vocation, location, and walk of life, when they forfeit the freedom that can be theirs. To keep your potential locked up is to look at the offer of all-encompassing liberation and say, "Thanks, but I think I'll pass."

May this never be said of you—or me.

May we instead be the kind of people who welcome our better, stronger, sturdier selves with arms opened wide—no excuses, no apologies, no regrets. In the coming pages, I'd like to show you how.

When working with partners and clients, my team's approach is to guide them through an intensive two-day Leadership Lab, which involves thoroughly, and at times painstakingly, introducing the key characteristics and tools of leadership, and showing them firsthand how to apply those tools to the most vexing problems they face. Invariably, the women and men who join us for these sessions leave energized and refreshed in their belief that they have the capacity to make a positive difference in their own lives, in the lives of others, and in their communities. They are emboldened to size up and solve future problems. And even more important, they are awakened to the potential inside themselves that has lain dormant for far too long.

They learn to recognize their power.

They learn to multiply that power.

And they learn to apply their power to bring about good in the world.

In so doing, they come alive.

I want *you* to come alive as well.

Here's what I've discovered: As you learn to harness the power within you, you will begin to make more sense out of life. You'll find that you really can patch up the brokenness of your past. You really can find purpose and meaning here and now. You really can make a positive impact on the world for decades to come.

It's time to stop unwittingly giving away your power. Choose to invest it, *on purpose*, instead.

The late great poet and playwright Maya Angelou never

fancied herself a writer in the traditional sense; but all that changed one night at a literary dinner party to which she had been invited by her friend the renowned author James Baldwin. Once the guests had enjoyed the meal together, talk turned to stories of each person's childhood. When Maya's turn came, she held the other guests in rapt attention with her lyrical stories. The hostess of the party was so entranced by Maya's experiences—and by the way she poetically depicted them—that she placed a call the following day to a publishing friend of hers.

"You ought to pursue this Maya Angelou!" the woman said to the publisher. And pursue her the publisher did. The result of that chance encounter at a dinner party was the release of Maya's first autobiographical work, *I Know Why the Caged Bird Sings*.

Not only did Maya Angelou experience what she referred to as great relief in "telling the truth" of her story, which tragically involved sexual, emotional, physical, and racial abuse, but she also helped liberate countless other young black women, who read Maya's book and felt understood—perhaps for the first time in their lives.

I had the privilege of serving alongside Ms. Angelou on the faculty of several conferences throughout the years, and the thought that she might never have had the opportunity to share both the revulsion and the redemption of her experience sends chills down my spine. What a colossal loss that would have been! Each time we crossed paths, I found her to be a woman of great composure and peace. After all she had been through in her life, it was amazing to behold.

Patching up our past brokenness brings solace to our

souls. You might say that is the backward-facing benefit of full-potential living. On top of that, the power that emerges from living out our full potential brings *purpose* to life today.

———

As I said earlier, the most profound outcome we see in clients who work through our two-day Leadership Lab is their growing realization that they possess potential far beyond what they thought or knew. I find it profoundly gratifying to see the testimonial videos our team shoots after the final Lab session and hear participants say something along the lines of "Until today, I had no idea how many resources were at my disposal for doing good in my home, in my job, and in the world. And who knew that those resources were *right here*, inside me, and in the people all around me, all along?" I experience a deep delight every time.

I love seeing people get unlocked and unleashed so they can connect with their true purpose in life. We are not here to be spectators. We are not here merely to acquire experiences and *stuff*. We are here to make a positive contribution so that we may leave this world a far better place than it was when we arrived. But we will never realize our purpose and our potential if we're stuck in a hole, in the dark, alone.

Stay with me; you're about to be beautifully *freed*.

———

Living to our full potential allows us to *promote an impact beyond ourselves*. Let's think for a moment about the most influential people we know, the mentor-types who loved us when we were unlovable; who invited us into the game when we were unskilled; who accepted us even after we failed; and who identified in us the capacity for good things. These high-impact people showed up instead of shrinking back. They lived big instead of playing it safe and small. And as a result, we were changed for the better.

When we choose to press into, not pull away from, our fullest potential, our influence goes well beyond *us*. We'll touch more on this point in part 3: "The Promise of the Path," but for now just be aware that the journey on which we're embarking is marked by *exponential impact*, as we learn to live joyfully beyond ourselves.

In a manner of speaking, this book is your very own Leadership Lab—not leadership as society defines it, which is according to title, position, and prestige; but leadership seen as solving problems and changing the order of things for the better. I have learned over and over that leaders are made, not born: We can *all* be leaders. We can influence others right where we are. We can learn to take our troubles in stride; and when we lie down at night, we can know that we embraced our potential that day . . . that we lived life to the fullest . . . that we flourished and thrived.

I should warn you that the journey to unlocking your potential won't follow a codified plan. In fact, the very first thing you need to do is become comfortable with a rather disconcerting idea: *As you journey toward who you are meant to be, you will not always know where you're going.*

chapter two

THE TRAGEDY OF THE TERMITE

Choosing the Path over the Plan

Despite a thousand other things that happened in my life between May 2015 and February 2016, the singular association I make with that ten-month span is that of running for president of the United States. I believe wholeheartedly in my reasons for entering the race—that *citizens*, not governments, are best able to effect lasting change; that power concentrated for too long in too few hands is destined to be abused; and that our country, just like each of its citizens, still has vast potential waiting to be tapped. But after a disappointing outcome in the New Hampshire primary, I knew that my campaign should end.

That night, my team and I flew back to Virginia in relative silence, weary from the months-long push. We landed just after one in the morning and went our separate ways. Nine hours later, I texted three of my staff members and invited them to my home to debrief the experience. I had awoken early as usual and went about my normal morning routine.

When my campaign manager, Frank Sadler, arrived, I opened the door, greeted him cheerfully, and said, "Well, I think we should get out now. No use belaboring things . . ."

Months later, Frank reflected on that day with a mutual friend of ours, and I was struck by his perspective. He said, "Here I was, totally devastated, after working our tails off for so long and then losing everything in one night, and Carly was totally *fine*.

"When I got home that night," he added, "I was a complete

wreck. And then, to make matters worse, I was agonizing over having to tell Carly the next morning that we needed to suspend our campaign. How was I going to position things? Moreover, how would she respond?"

Frank said he stood at my front door for a full minute before ringing the bell, dreading the conversation he knew we needed to have. When he finally rang, and I opened the door, he was shocked by what he saw.

"There she was, looking perfectly put together, smiling from ear to ear, her dogs happily wagging their tails as they stood at her side, and all I could think was *Don't you understand what happened last night? Don't you know what this means? How can you be okay?*"

Of course, I understood exactly what had transpired, and what it meant for all of us. I had given the race my best energy, my best intentions, my best passion, and my most creative thought, all while keeping my character intact. To step away from the presidential race was simply the next right decision to make. It wasn't a failure. It wasn't cause for devastation, grief, or regret. To think that way would be handing my power over to emotions that would never pay me back. I had begun my campaign knowing the odds were very long indeed. Of course I was sad that I hadn't won. But I would learn from this leg of the journey and move forward, just as I'd always done.

"What will you do now?" the media outlets all wanted to know after the suspension of my presidential campaign. I told them I would seize the next right opportunity for making a contribution that would count.

Those were more than mere words to me; that was my intention, through and through.

Seize the next right opportunity for making a contribution that will count.

It may seem odd or even neglectful, but the truth of my situation is that I've never had "a plan." I've never staked my success on a dream. I've never hung my hat on a destination that I was determined to get to someday. The reason I had no trouble "getting over" the way my presidential run panned out is that, while I was always prepared to win and do the job, I was also always prepared to lose and do something else that would change the order of things for the better.

Given the way my story has turned out thus far, almost every audience I address finds it entertaining that I majored in medieval history and philosophy in college, not in business administration, political science, or even marketing. They're amused because they understand that at the end of my expensive four years as an undergrad at Stanford, I was essentially all dressed up with nowhere to go. I had my degree from a top school, but no real purpose or prospects.

But it wasn't until after my botched attempt at law school that it really hit me: I had no plan for my life. What *was* I going to do?

My only answer to that question was, "Go get a job," and I shifted my focus to simply earning an income—*any* income—doing just about anything.

I signed on with Kelly Services, where I had temped during college summers, and resumed my role as a "Kelly Girl," a moniker that today would be politically incorrect. Still, during its rise to prominence beginning in the late 1940s, the Kelly organization provided women an on-ramp to a workforce dominated by men. In 1977, I desperately craved a way in.

The company that hired me was a nine-person real-estate brokerage in Palo Alto, called Marcus and Millichap. A receptionist had left, so that became my new gig: answering phones, filing paperwork, typing up contracts, distributing mail. It wasn't the most stimulating work, but it was steady, and I was determined to do my job with excellence and dedication.

Decades later, I would look back on that decision and see that it had made all the difference for me. Today, when young people or their parents ask me for a single piece of advice, my answer is always the same: "Get a job. Any job. Do that job with excellence. You will learn a lot about yourself. You will learn a lot about other people. And opportunity will knock. Be brave enough to walk through the door when it does."

A woman I spoke to recently recounted for me the early days of her career.

"When I got my start, I was twenty-one years old, just out of college, and thrilled to have a real job."

She was hired as a marketing assistant at a small consulting firm—sixty employees at its peak—and despite the low-level nature of the job, she reported to the senior vice president of marketing, a woman in her fifties.

"During one of my performance reviews," she said, "my boss told me, 'What you need is a mission. A vision. A *goal*. Instead of letting life happen to you, *you* need to happen to *life*.'"

The VP went on to counsel her young charge to set specific compensation goals as her objective.

"Always strive to make a multiple of the decade you're in," the boss explained. "So, when you're in your twenties, make twice your age in thousands. When you're in your thirties, make three times your age. In your forties, four times your age. And on and on, like that."

As I listened to this woman articulate the VP's plan, I couldn't help but think how much money most retirees would be making by now if they had only known how to employ this approach. Six times sixty-five years in thousands is a salary most people would be fine with, I think.

"In addition to the salary specifications," my new friend continued, "she alerted me to *title* concerns. If I hoped to be taken seriously someday, I should push for vice president or senior vice president," she said.

"I was still entry-level, Carly! This was incredibly stressful news."

This woman is now a successful business owner (by anyone's standard), despite taking not an ounce of her former boss's advice. And as I studied her face and her demeanor, I detected the same sense of freedom that I myself had felt when I'd looked my dad in the eye and told him I was quitting law school. There was peace there—a settled confidence. There was the satisfaction of having gone her own way. She and I had both taken a pass on life-as-destination, choosing instead a more soul-enriching journey.

Let me come at this from a different angle for a moment. When I was fifteen years old, my father, then a professor of law, loaded up my family and relocated us to Ghana, West Africa. The government of Ghana had recently adopted a new constitution, and my father thought it would be all sorts of fun to teach Ghanaian law students how to understand, interpret, and apply their new laws. So off we went.

Soon after our arrival, as we made our way by car to our new living quarters, I asked our host about the giant mounds that dotted the landscape. Were they hills? I wondered. He chuckled and said in his thick, lilting accent, "No, no . . . those are termite mounds."

He explained that all those termites did, day in and day out, was trudge along, heads down, moving dirt from one end of the mound to the other. "They go like that all the time," he said, "moving around and around, clearing the same old dirt."

Then our host laughed and said something I've remembered to this day: "You know, people can be a lot like termites, can't they?"

After some reflection, I think what he meant was that we can all fall into a rut, keeping our heads down and our eyes on the dirt, staying extremely busy doing meaningless activity.

I think those termite hills were an apt depiction of what happens to too many of us. Other people's expectations can get us into a rut. In our society, everyone assumes that a *destination* is what we all need. Success means having our lives planned out.

One example: As every high school senior can attest, a trio of questions awaits them:

- "Where are you going to college?"
- "What are you going to major in?"
- "*Then* what will you do?"

Back when they were eighteen years old themselves, very few of the people posing these questions had any idea how to answer them; but still, they ask. And each time those questions come up, it reinforces a cultural norm that says, "There is a required system here, in case you hadn't noticed. You need to set your sights on a specific diploma earned from a specific institution that will prepare you for a specific occupation, if you ever hope to truly succeed."

What those unsuspecting high school seniors don't know yet is that they will be handed another set of questions upon graduation from college.

- "Congratulations on your graduation! Where are you going to work?"
- "What job are you hoping to get?"
- "How will you move up the ranks from there?"
- *"What is your five-year plan?"*

The poor graduates think, *I thought I'd answered all the big questions already. You mean to tell me there are more?*

Indeed, there are *always* more. In our culture, such questions abound.

For people who are dating: "When are you going to get married?"

For those who get married: "When will you start having kids?"

For the parents of a toddler: "Any siblings on the way?"

And before you know it, we're answering the same series of questions about the next generation.

"Where will your kids go to college?"

"Did your daughter get the job?"

"Is your son dating anyone seriously?"

"Any weddings on the horizon?"

"Any grandkids yet?"

On and on it goes; where it stops, nobody knows.

Actually, you and I both know: It *doesn't* stop, unless we *make* it stop.

I vote for making it stop.

———

It's natural to fall into a rut from time to time, where we wonder what we're doing, where we're going, and how it will all pan out in the end. Sometimes we know how we got there—a key relationship broke apart, a big push toward a goal came to an end, a milestone birthday showed up—and sometimes we have no clue how or why life seems to have ground to a halt. Either way, our instinct in these situations is to find a way out of that rut. Not knowing what else to do, and not wanting to go the way of the tragic termite, we snap our fingers and hatch a plan.

"I know what will fix this," we say. "I'll just get a new job!"

"I'll move to a new city!"

"I'll start dating again!"

"I just need a new challenge! A new adventure! A tighter set of abs."

We focus on that "one thing"—whatever it is—convinced in our hearts and minds that *it* will get us going again. But that one thing, though perhaps alluring, isn't magical. There is only so much that a new direction can accomplish. The dirty little secret of a "destination mind-set"—of living life *on plan*—is that it fails to deliver what it promises. Not just occasionally, but *every time*. Having a plan promises success and certainty, promotion and stability, status and *cash*. But as I've seen countless times firsthand, it delivers the very opposite. For those who adopt an *on-plan* approach to life, there are only three outcomes possible:

- You get there, but you can't sustain it.
- You get there, but it can't sustain you.
- You never get there at all.

Each outcome is devastating in its own way.

Some destination-minded people arrive at their goals—the title, the office, the salary—but are unable to maintain the measures of success they sought so desperately. A high-level executive I know, who worked for more than two decades to earn the title of CEO, comes to mind. During a guest-lecture he gave for a class I took at MIT, he said he knew when he was twenty-eight that he would reach his goal. To his credit, he eventually did. They handed him the key to the corner office suite, introduced him to the pilot of his private jet, and gave him stock options as if they were sticks of gum, on top of an eight-figure salary.

To all appearances, he was living the dream. Everything looked perfect. But behind the scenes, a different reality began to emerge. Because of how he had bulldozed his way to the top, his senior team didn't respect him, his staff barely knew him, and the company's board couldn't hold him accountable. Within three years, his grand dream had turned into a nightmare, and he was cut loose. I think the official reason given for his dismissal was "neglecting to pivot effectively with the ever-changing industry" or some such nonsense, but the truth was plain to see. He'd bullied his way into the corner office, and like most bullies, he was eventually exposed.

I think of a young woman who longed to get married and did, only to blow up her marriage several years later with chronically uncontrolled spending habits.

I think of a pastor who worked tirelessly to build a congregation of thousands of people, only to detonate the whole deal by engaging inappropriately with a member of the congregation he was there to serve.

I think of a high school senior who earned a full ride to a prestigious university, only to forfeit the money after her first year by partying more than she cracked the books.

There are kids who make the leap from youth sports to the star-studded reality of pro sports, only to squander the opportunity they've been given by living large.

There are gamblers who hit the jackpot, only to fritter away their fortune.

In recent years, we've learned of broadcasters who finally earned the coveted anchor's chair, actors who soared to the top of their craft, politicians who rose to positions of influence, and studio heads who could bankroll any film they desired, only to have their true colors finally kick them right out the door.

When you hyperfixate on a destination, you might indeed succeed at doing what you always wanted to do. But what kind of person will you be once you arrive? I've seen it time and again: The depth of integrity required to sustain a position of influence—in any forum, in any industry, in any role—is often shortchanged by compromises made on the way up.

————

Another unfortunate outcome of living "on plan" is that you reach your destination but it can't sustain you. Novelist Gertrude Stein's observation about the razing of her childhood home—"there is no *there* there"[1]— perfectly sums up this result. You set your sights on a destination and move intently toward it, only to realize soon after you arrive that it isn't all it was cracked up to be.

If you follow pro football, you may remember seeing Steve Kroft's *60 Minutes* interview with Tom Brady following the third of Brady's six Super Bowl victories. Despite all the money, fame, and unparalleled achievements the quarterback had racked up, something still felt "off."

In a moment of candor, Brady said, "Why do I have three Super Bowl rings and still think there's something greater out there for me? I mean, maybe a lot of people would say, 'Hey, man, this is *what it is*—I reached my goal, my dream; my life is—' Me? I think, 'It's gotta be more than this . . .'"

"What's the answer?" Kroft asked.

"I wish I knew! I wish I knew."[2]

We think there's a tremendous *there* there, don't we, at the height where we've set our sights. At one point in my own life, attaining the "law-school graduate" label that my father so highly esteemed was the pinnacle of my aspirations. We're just *sure* there's a *there* up there, aren't we? Yet, soon after our glorious arrival, we find we've been duped.

The third unfortunate outcome of an "on-plan" approach to life is that you never get there at all. You work and struggle and strive, but somehow you just never arrive at your destination.

Whenever we chose to chase a destination—whether we wind up reaching it or not—something is *wrong* in our lives. My contention is this: If you've ever caught yourself thinking, "When I get _____, *then* I'll _____," you've fallen prey to "the plan."

"When I get the promotion, *then* I'll be taken seriously."

"When I get married, *then* I'll be fulfilled."

"When I get the multiple-of-my-age salary, *then* I will have arrived."

When I/then I—it ought to be categorized as a certifiable drug. Common side effects include debilitating anxiety, pervasive insecurity, and inexplicable fits of rage. Has been linked to plummeting self-confidence, rampant narcissism, deep depression, and an emotionally and spiritually fatal termite-like condition known as Dig, Dig, Dig, Dig, Dig.

Truth be told, signing up for "the plan" really *is* dangerous business, and such side effects are truer than we know. Why? Because if we reach our destination but can't maintain our position there, we're prone to self-destruction; if we reach our destination but find it unfulfilling and not as we'd hoped, we wrestle with paralyzing disillusionment; and if we fail to ever reach our destination at all, we suffer despair that can take us down fast. At some point, these destinations take on a life of their own and start controlling the process we mistakenly believed *we* were directing.

None of these broken options represents the life we were made to live; to me, none of these sounds like *success*. My recommendation, as you have likely gathered by now, is to ditch the plan once and for all. But if we forsake the destination mind-set, what do we set our minds on now? If we agree that "pursuing the plan" is the wrong way to go, then what *should* we pursue? Let's turn our attention to those important questions. I think the answers will encourage your heart.

I mentioned that during my receptionist days at the brokerage firm, I had no real direction in mind. And though I had no interest in pursuing my father's dream for me to become a lawyer, there was a distinct part of his legacy that I *was* interested in fleshing out. There were two important qualities that my dad greatly prized and thus emulated beautifully throughout his life.

"Hard work and excellence," he'd say. "If you do nothing else, do those two things."

So I decided to put into practice my dad's two priorities. I arrived a few minutes early each day and stayed a few minutes late. I cordially greeted every person who entered our lobby, and I tried to meet their needs with kindness and respect. I refused to indulge any workplace drama, instead speaking well of everyone. I created new, more effective systems for little things and saw that they had a big effect. I behaved as if I were grateful for that position—and, in fact, I truly was. I was honest in my conversations. I was encouraging toward the other staff. I was teachable when my boss gave me suggestions. I did everything I could to be an asset to the team.

And all that time I was utterly aimless. *I had no clue what I wanted to do with my life.*

Six months into my time at the firm, two of the partners approached me and said, "Carly, we can't help but notice how hard you're working . . . how much of an innovator you are . . . how much potential you clearly have. Would you be interested in watching what we do in the brokerage world and training to do similar work?"

Why, yes, I would *be interested in that. I'd be* very *interested in that.*

Though I never became a broker, I fell in love with business—a world I had not known much about. I liked the teamwork of it, the focus on actual results, the interactions with paying customers. Because these two men saw potential in me and introduced me to their world, and because of their continued encouragement, I eventually enrolled in and completed an MBA program, which eventually led to my being hired by AT&T in their Washington, DC, office as an "account executive"—a puffed-up title for an entry-level salesperson—which my father blissfully regarded as "successful enough" that he never brought up the law-school debacle again.

It was at AT&T that I first realized it isn't so bad to not have a plan. I wasn't *trying* not to have a plan; *I just didn't have one.* I was so far from planned, in fact, that I never joined the (quite generous) employee savings plan. Big, big, big mistake. (Maybe sometimes it's okay to have a plan.)

Every time I am introduced to a group, the inevitable résumé reading ensues: "She joined AT&T as an entry-level salesperson. Ten years later, she became an officer of the company. She was then asked to lead the Lucent Technologies spin-off, the largest IPO in history at that time. In 1999, she became the first woman to lead a company in the Fortune 50 by becoming the CEO of HP."

It sounds like a nice, smooth trajectory, with the corner office in mind and a plan firmly in place every step of the way. Nothing could be further from the truth.

During Q&As, business school audiences always ask when I knew I'd be a CEO. I always reply, "The day I accepted the job at HP."

The truth is, there never was a plan. What there was instead was a *path*. A path of hard work and commitment to excellence, no matter the circumstances. A path of running toward problems instead of away from them. A path of unlocking the potential of others by collaborating with them to change the order of things. A path of recognizing opportunity when it knocks and having the courage to walk through the door.

When we're not fixated on our plans for the future, we're free to focus our attention on the view from where we are.

You see, when we're not fixated on our plans for the future, we're free to focus our attention on the view from where we are. Instead of putting our heads down and staying in our ruts, we can actually see the people around us, the problems around us, the opportunities around us to make a positive contribution and change things for the better. We need to shift from the fretfulness of living *on plan* to the fulfillment of living *on path*.

We stay on path by adhering to a set of fully controllable character traits that prepare us from the inside out to seize the right opportunities at the right time with the requisite confidence, wisdom, and poise. The path to our full potential is a journey toward increased readiness for living the life we were made to live. Since I have been on this path, my life has been filled with accomplishment, yes, but also adventure, love, grace, joy, and positive contribution.

And yet . . . my life has also had its share of heartbreak, tragedy, pain, sorrow, and disappointment. For all of us, it is the nature of life to ebb and flow. The path doesn't promise that times will always be good, decisions will always be easy, or outcomes will never disappoint us.

The reason I was truly fine when my campaign manager, Frank Sadler, stood on my doorstep dreading the conversation he knew we needed to have the morning after the New Hampshire primary was that *my feet were still firmly planted on the path.* Had I attached my self-worth to winning the nomination—not to mention the presidency—I would have been thrown off course. Instead, I stood up, dusted myself off, and put one foot in front of the other, moving forward again . . . always forward.

And in the same way that Frank eyed me with a hint of suspicion that morning, the people around you may raise an eyebrow or two when you begin to find your way. When you get this reaction, my advice is to *keep on keepin' on.* Remind yourself that you can suffer some tough blows without getting completely knocked out—in fact, you can gain strength and wisdom, and even be blessed by those tough blows. You can stare down your struggles and emerge victorious. You can endure all the twists and turns in the road without becoming disoriented or distraught.

I've always loved the word *vicissitudes*—first, because it's so fun to say. But more meaningfully because it captures the variations, fluctuations, and deviations that make our lives remarkable, our seasons memorable, and our years distinct one from the next.

You can live in such a way that the vicissitudes of life will fuel your journey.

Here's my promise to you: You really can live in such a way that the vicissitudes of life won't flatten you; in fact, they will *fuel* your journey.

You can be known for your steadiness.

You can be known for your sturdiness.

You can be known for bringing peace into any room.

You can exhibit kindness and graciousness and conviction and strength.

You can change *everything* for the better, simply by showing up.

You can find your way and never lose it again.

chapter three

WHAT'S WRONG IS ALSO WHAT'S RIGHT

Problems as Pavement under Your Feet

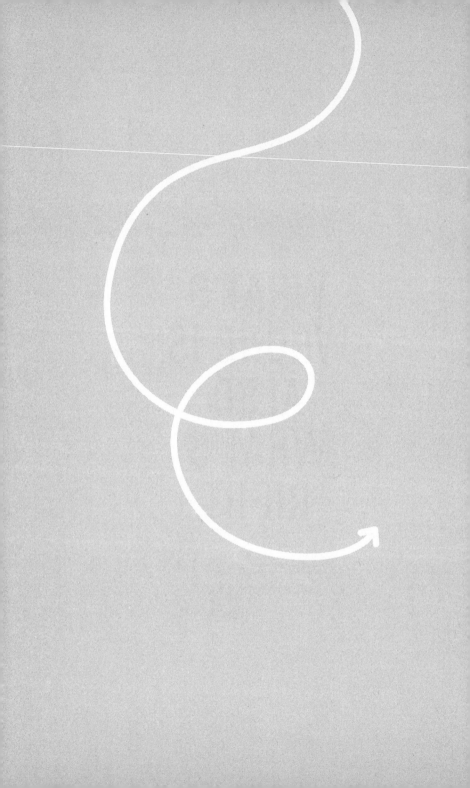

AT THIS POINT, I hope you're asking a question: *So, how do I find this path?*

It's a good question, a necessary question, a logical question. People are always relieved when I assure them that finding the path requires no magic tricks, no group-therapy classes, no exotic rituals, and no games. In fact, the path is right in front of you, every single day, and the way to find it is very straightforward: *Find a problem to solve.*

That's it.

Find a meaningful problem that is close to you, that affects you, that matters to you, and work to solve it.

Problems are the pavement on the path of life. Problem solving is what tells you you're finding your way.

What's *wrong* in your immediate context can also be what's *right* for you.

An illustration may help to reinforce this idea.

In my part of the country, the most prominent natural feature is one of the world's longest footpaths, the renowned Appalachian Trail. This winding path, which spans almost twenty-two hundred miles across fourteen states, from Georgia to Maine—including Virginia, where I live—is thought to be visited by more than two million people annually. Some are on the trek of their lives, while others are simply out for a day hike. But whatever brings these hikers to the trail, and regardless of how long they stay, one constant that makes their experience far more predictable is the famed "trail blazes."

Positioned all along the trail, these broad brushstrokes of white paint on more than 165,000 tree trunks, posts, and rocks tell hikers that, no matter how dense the forest has become or how isolated things may feel on the long stretches of trail between aid stations, they are still on the path. In a similar way, the problems we encounter in life, love, and work are the confirmation we need that we're still on the path after all.

Whenever organizations enlist the help of my foundation, Unlocking Potential, it's because *they have problems they want to get solved.* A series of communication breakdowns or branding inconsistencies or operational complexities have them tied up in knots, and their hope is that a few days spent with our Leadership Lab curriculum will have a certain untangling effect.

Sometimes people hope we will show up with the answers to their problems. Instead, we tell them they have everything they need to solve the problems themselves. Our job is to give them the tools, the coaching, the practice, so they can become more effective leaders, collaborators, and problem solvers.

Problems are part of every organization and every life. "Everything is fine" is always a myth. However, when people or organizations focus on the right problems, and work to solve them instead of simply ignoring or complaining about them, they are on the path.

"Focusing on the right problems means you're on the path," I remind our clients countless times throughout our days together. Solving problems isn't just the payoff for leadership done well; it's also the payoff for *life* done well.

When I first joined AT&T, I noticed problems everywhere I went. Big problems and small problems, consequential problems and incidental problems, problems that were isolated to a specific work team and problems that affected us all. Some of the problems, I'd later learn, had existed for years, and yet there they sat, unresolved. Other problems were fresh and new, but they wreaked havoc all the same.

As I mentioned earlier, I had no real business or leadership experience at this point. I had zero knowledge of the telecommunications industry. I had never managed anyone or anything in my life. This terrible trifecta led me to believe I had no power. I was a lone, unqualified woman in a sea of male experts in a complex industry. It would have been easy just to keep my head down, hoping to survive another day without my inadequacies being exposed. But those pesky problems kept beckoning me.

Shouldn't somebody do *something about those issues?*

A watershed moment came when I realized why problems so frequently fester. It's not because people don't see them. It's not because people aren't affected by them. It's not even because people don't care. And it certainly isn't because no one has any idea about how to make things better. It is because status quo—the way things are, and the way things have always been—has great power.

Why is the current state so powerful? Because some people prefer the known to the unknown. Some are invested in the way things are, so they prefer to live with problems unsolved. They don't want anything to change.

But here's the thing: For every person who is invested in keeping things the way they are, there are just as many, maybe more, who know what might be done to fix the problem—to make things *better*. In fact, I've learned time and again that the people closest to the problem, the ones most affected by the problem, always—*always*—have some good ideas about how to solve the problem. But often they're not asked, or they aren't given the opportunity, or they don't seize the opportunity because they don't know how much power they possess to upset the status quo. I learned that when I included the people who understood the situation, when I collaborated with them and supported them, together we were able to change the order of things for the better and solve the problem.

A conversation with an engineer named Jim comes to mind just now. He was one of those guys who fly below the radar most of the time. Every day, he arrived at work at the same time, parked in the same slot, ate lunch by himself at his desk, and departed at closing time, without causing a single stir. People looked past Jim; he kind of blended in that way. Most people would have described him as steady but unremarkable, dependable but average.

Because I had only recently become Jim's boss, I didn't know much about engineering, and I didn't know much about Jim. So one day I sat down and asked him to tell me about his job and what he did. And I asked him if he saw any problems in his work each day.

Jim eyed me for a moment, as if weighing whether to divulge what was on his mind.

"Well," he began, "there is something I've been wondering about . . ."

Jim designed circuits, and every month AT&T got billed for those circuits.

"I've noticed," he said, "that the circuit manufacturer's bills never exactly reflect the designs I provide."

"Well, what do you think we ought to do about that?" I asked.

"I think we ought to check 'em," Jim said.

I asked Jim to start checking those invoices. I secured resources for him so he could check them more thoroughly and more regularly. And lo and behold, Jim was right; we were being mischarged—and not by a little. Correcting those billing errors saved AT&T $300 million the first year alone.

In a later chapter, we'll talk about the power of collaboration—which certainly was evident here. But for now, let me direct your attention to the fundamentals of what transpired. Jim was aware of the problem. He assumed, having raised the issue previously with no response, that no one was interested in solving it. Status quo was the way it was. When I came in search of problems, the problem was brought to light, clarified, and worked on. And eventually the problem was solved.

Solving that problem—a *massive* win for our team— not only saved the company millions of dollars, but it also deepened Jim's organizational credibility with his superiors, garnered additional support and respect from his peers, broadened his appreciation for the complexities of how things worked outside of his direct role, and increased his sense of self-confidence. The solving of this one immediate problem prepared Jim to solve even *bigger* problems in days to come. Problems are what pave the path to our full potential. Solving problems is what enables us to thrive.

I have learned over the years that if I am not actively solving a problem somewhere, then I am not stretching, learning, or experiencing growth. The reason is that opportunities for growth always hide behind the problems we see. As we do when eating a Tootsie Pop, we have to break through that hard outer shell to get to the good stuff in the middle.

We find a delightful depiction of this idea in Kobi Yamada's charming children's book titled *What Do You Do with a Problem?* The main character, a grade-school-age boy, awakens one morning to discover he has a problem—portrayed in the book as an ominous dark cloud that swirls above his head. The boy didn't *want* this problem or *ask* for this problem or *like* this problem, but there it is.

As most people would do in response to a problem, the little boy tries everything in his power to make it go away. "I shooed it," he says. "I scowled at it. I tried ignoring it. But nothing worked."[1] Still, the problem remains. And then it grows even larger. The little boy begins to fret: What if his problem starts to eclipse everything else in his life? What if it swallows him up?

As the book progresses, the dark cloud grows and grows, until it eventually engulfs the page. By now the boy has *had* it. He simply can't live like this! So he decides to quit worrying and start solving his problem instead. He gets out a quill pen, an inkwell, a blank sheet of blotter paper, and a T square. With a bead of sweat trickling down his face, he plots a thorough course. He strategizes and schemes and tests and refines, until he is ready for the momentous event. He will take on this problem with all his might. He will conquer it. He will *win*.

Next, the little boy, fittingly wearing aviator goggles, leaps into the sky, stretches his arms wide, and attacks the problem head-on. And then he makes the most amazing discovery: There is something *inside* that big, dark cloud. "My problem held an opportunity!" the boy says joyfully. "It was an opportunity for me to learn and to grow. To be brave. To do something."[2]

The final page of the book shows the boy and his friends, faces to the wind, unafraid of future problems that may come. That little boy knows the truth of things, and at such a tender age! Problems can be friends, if we'll regard them as such. We can befriend them instead of begrudging them. We can welcome them in rather than push them away.

If you're like most people I meet, all this talk of "befriending problems" has you riddled with internal angst. Indeed, our tendency when we encounter problems is not exactly to rejoice. Grumble? Yes. Gripe? Of course. Gossip to anyone who will lend an ear? These are reflexive responses when troubles come our way. Running *toward* problems? Not so much. We tend to run away from them instead. Which is why, despite our griping and grumbling, our circumstances stay fixed, we remain frustrated, and not a single problem is solved.

It's uncanny, isn't it, how deeply we long to set our faces to the wind like that little boy in the book, unafraid of the future, even as we stay stubbornly stuck in the mud of our current dilemmas, annoyed by our sorry lot. What is it that keeps us from applying our best energies, our best efforts, our best ideas to resolve the issues that have us tied up in knots? What keeps us coasting on yesterday's knowledge and yesterday's solutions, sliding backward instead of moving ahead?

I have learned that, despite talking a very good game, many people don't want to solve problems. Don't get me wrong—*they want the problems solved.* But they don't want to do what it takes to solve them.

A lot of these people can be found in politics. I find it interesting and fascinating that a country whose government was originally intended to promote citizen legislators wound up with career politicians instead. When our country was in its infancy, our leaders hoped that teachers or doctors or business owners or farmers or lawyers who were interested in bettering the nation would take a brief hiatus—at most, several years—from their vocations to serve in an elected capacity in DC. (Did I mention the hiatus was to be *brief*?) By setting up shop in DC and never going back to ordinary citizen life, today's politicians signal to the rest of us that they don't really want to solve problems and make progress. If they wanted to solve problems, they would solve problems.

Though it might be fun to point fingers at our government officials and blame them for hemming and hawing and dragging their feet, the reality is that politics lives downstream of culture. What "we the people" buy into, our politicians will one day believe. What "we the people" prioritize, our politicians will one day prize. What "we the people" declare, our politicians will one day espouse. The only blame to be doled out, then, belongs to you and me. If our political system fails to provide effective, efficient problem solving, it's only because *we* failed in problem solving first—beginning with our failure to solve the problem of career politicians. The reason for our lack of success is simple and quite apparent: The problem with problems is that *something's gotta change* in order to bring the necessary resolution. Solving problems is one thing, but people *don't like change.*

Change! Such a troubling word. Such a troubling *concept.* I often say that change is a lot like heaven: Everybody wants to go there, but nobody wants to die. Change requires a death of sorts—a death of the *status quo.* But just as so much of nature must lie dormant and fallow each winter before springtime can show off her blooms, you and

> Change requires a death of sorts— a death of the status quo.

I will never achieve new levels of efficiency, effectiveness, and expertise—that latent potential we desperately long to see realized—without first being willing to *kill* some things.

Stale thinking comes to mind.

Thoughtless communication.

Rampant cynicism.

Inadequate follow-through.

And then there's indulgent self-promotion—oh, do I have opinions about *that*!

Happiness researcher Gretchen Rubin insists that there is a directly proportional relationship between what she calls "outer order" and "inner calm." In the same way that my simple, uncluttered workspace at Unlocking Potential allows my mind to think clearly about the problems I'm working to solve, if you will put to death the unhelpful attitudes, actions, and patterns of speech that have cluttered your world for too long, you will see plainly how to address even the most vexing of dilemmas. *You will boldly march up the path.*

Let me share some insight I've gained that I hope will inform the rest of your life: Full-potential people are those who change the order of things for the better. They treat this singular objective as number one on their job description.

Change the order of things for the better . . . and things will get better.

This is true within a corporate structure, an educational environment, an at-home setting, a nonprofit sector, or a freelancer space. It's true no matter who you are. The impact you crave by living at maximum potential will be realized only by solving real problems that affect real people. By proactively changing the order of things for the better, day by day, you will gradually—and sometimes suddenly—make a positive difference. Likewise, if you come across people who gripe a lot but refuse to solve the problems they're griping about, people who refuse to change the order of things, then you have people who are *choosing* to live below their potential—that is, until they change their unwillingness to change.

What, then, keeps us from shifting and changing and solving the problems that need to be solved? I've noticed four common pitfalls people tumble into that keep them from solving the problems they say they want solved. These snares hinder forward movement. See which one you're most prone to fall into, and then we'll look at how you can steer clear.

Pitfall 1: Presumption of Innocence

Key theme: Abdication
Motto: "Not my problem."

The first pitfall, *presumption of innocence*, is marked by lack of engagement and a refusal to take responsibility. We refer to it somewhat humorously in the words of a Polish proverb: *"Nie mój cyrk, nie moje małpy"*—"not my circus; not my monkeys."

As it relates to problem solving, we adopt the presumption-of-innocence approach whenever we distance ourselves from a dilemma that we are fully equipped to help solve. We see the problem. We understand the problem. We grasp the effects that the problem has caused. We just have no desire to get messy by engaging the problem firsthand, so we dust off our hands and move on.

Jim the engineer, my colleague at AT&T who saved the company millions of dollars by catching the invoice snafu, certainly could have presumed innocence by claiming—rightly so—that the issue belonged to the accounting team, not to him. He could have turned a blind eye to the problem, kept his head down, and simply tended to "the work he was paid to do." Thankfully, he didn't. Thankfully, he stepped around this pitfall and stayed on the path toward his full potential.

A story that broke in April 2018 involved Austin Perine, of Birmingham, Alabama, who had been buying Burger

King chicken sandwiches by the dozen to pass out to people who are homeless in his part of town. What makes this story remarkable is that Austin Perine is four years old. Austin's dad wanted his young son to understand what homelessness looked like, so he took him to a local shelter, where women and men were waiting in line for a hot meal. Austin took one look around and asked his dad, "Can we feed them?"

Austin began using his weekly allowance to purchase hot sandwiches—instead of buying himself a new toy—and then traipsed about town with his father in tow, looking for hungry mouths to feed. Today's social-media trends being what they are, Burger King soon learned of Austin's efforts and decided to donate $1,000 a month for a year to fund Austin's altruistic work. Now, he and his dad are dreaming of opening a shelter of their own, one that addresses not just the physical needs involved in homelessness, but the emotional and mental health needs as well.[3]

I think we'd all understand if Austin whiled away his days eating Popsicles and playing with trucks. He's *four*. But though he may not yet have the verbal acuity to express it, he has picked up on something that is utterly changing the course of his life: We cannot reach our full potential, and enjoy the satisfaction of that journey, unless we invest ourselves in solving a problem somewhere.

Your problem might be a boss who can't seem to make a decision.

It might be a broken relationship that matters deeply to you.

It might be your seeming inability to manage your finances.

It might be your neighbor's barking dogs.

As in Austin's case, it might be seeing the same hungry people around your town, day after day after day.

The *proximity* of a problem is far more important than its *parameters*. I have long held that the people closest to the problem are best suited to solve it. In other words, if a problem is keeping you up at night, *it's likely your problem to solve.*

Pitfall 2: Rush to Judgment

Key theme: Misidentification
Motto: "I've got *just* the solution for that."

The second pitfall, *rush to judgment*, is marked by presumption and pride. We stumble into this pitfall whenever we think we know how to solve a problem without taking the time to assess it from all angles and accurately identify the source rather than just the symptoms. If we treat the symptoms of a problem but not the problem itself, we end up solving nothing at all.

Politicians in Washington, DC, are guilty of this every day, year after year and decade after decade. Rather than asking the people closest to the problem how they might choose to solve it, and then providing them with the resources and encouragement and power to do so, they tell us that *they* know the right answer and will take care of it, if only we will reelect them and send them more money. But between the politicians, the lobbyists, and the bureaucrats, the problems only seem to fester and the powers that be in Washington only get stronger—which might have been their real goal all along. Remember the power of the status quo?

Real problems in the real world are rarely simple enough

to be solved with a flippant "Oh, I've got *just* the solution for that!" Real problems require a real investment of time and thoughtful, clear-eyed assessment, as the prospective problem solvers dig deep under the surface to excavate the source of the pain, and thus the best solution to pursue. The reason people closest to the problem—those who are most affected by the problem—are best able to solve it is that they are usually the ones prepared to invest the time and energy to *understand* the problem.

An old children's fable comes to mind that perfectly portrays this idea.

As the story goes, there once was a king who ruled a prosperous kingdom filled with happy, successful people. One day, he decided to visit the people he ruled. He went near and far, even to remote places his chariot couldn't take him. In those places, he went on foot.

Walking long distances proved to be very enjoyable for the king, as he was better able to see what was happening in his kingdom and engage the people in unhurried conversations. But as the days went by, the king noticed a distinct pain radiating from his right leg.

"I wish to keep walking," the king said to himself, "but this pain is intolerable."

The king went to his ministers and complained that something must be done at once to make the kingdom's roads more comfortable for him to tread.

"The paths are so jagged and stony that my leg is suffering!" he declared. "But I have *just* the solution for that."

The king ordered that all the roads in the kingdom be

paved with soft, supple leather. That would ease his footfalls, he reasoned. Yes, this was the right thing to do.

The ministers were shocked by the king's decree. How many of the kingdom's cattle would have to be slaughtered to provide enough leather for this effort? How expensive a proposition would this prove to be? And yet they did not object.

One of the king's ministers, who lived in the neighborhoods the king had visited on foot, approached him with a different idea. Kneeling before the king, he took a measurement of the king's foot. A few days later, he returned with a pair of shoes made of the same soft, supple leather the king had ordered as pavement throughout the kingdom.

"There," said the king's minister. "Now you may go wherever you wish in comfort."

The king applauded the minister's wise ways, and all in the kingdom lived happily, and comfortably, ever after.

Pitfall 3: Failure to Launch

Key theme: Procrastination
Motto: "I don't know where to start."

A third problem-solving pitfall is *failure to launch*. This pitfall occurs when problems are kicked down the road because the solution is not immediately obvious or the person lacks the will to overcome inertia and get started. The toll that procrastination takes on our financial, emotional, psychological, and relational well-being is significant. Though some people probably do work better "under pressure," the risks of procrastination tend to outweigh any benefits. Procrastinators sap

Problems are what pave the path to our full potential. Solving problems is what enables us to thrive.

energy from an organization as tasks remain "in progress" for longer than necessary. Procrastination causes people to rush through tasks at the last minute, compromising thoughtful creativity and thoroughness. But perhaps the most damaging consequence of procrastination is that it can cause us to miss wonderful opportunities for connection, advancement, and that sense of accomplishment that comes with seeing a problem through to the end.

The CEO of Unlocking Potential, Casey Enders, is a bright, witty woman who loves to interact with people, invest in friendships, and create inviting spaces where meaningful conversations can unfold. But with a busy work life and an intense travel schedule, she can be tempted to allow her longing for deep connection to go unmet.

She and her husband are first-time homeowners, and upon moving in, Casey realized it was going to be difficult to host guests in their cozy house unless they limited their entertaining to one or two visitors at a time. Then she had an idea. If they did something about their "atrocious backyard," as she described it, they would gain additional space for entertaining, and thereby scratch the itch for interpersonal connection that she always feels.

Knowing Casey as I do, I wasn't surprised to learn that she immediately translated the goal into a project, complete with line-item expenses, a detailed prioritization of tasks with due dates, and a compelling vision to keep her motivated each step of the way.

"I would love to host a Memorial Day barbecue in our backyard," she said. "*That* would be the bomb."

Though it would have been easy to let such a problem go

unresolved for weeks or months, and then push it off until next spring, or even the spring after that, Casey chose a different tack. She knew that creating a welcoming environment would compel her to extend frequent invitations for friends and loved ones to swing by. In this case, solving a seemingly simple problem—and doing it now, not later—beautifully addressed a complex need.

Mary Todd Lincoln once wrote in a letter to a friend, "That most difficult of all problems to solve, my evil genius Procrastination has whispered me to tarry til a more convenient season."[4]

Thankfully, we can whisper back, "*No*."

Pitfall 4: Scarcity Mentality

Key theme: Resignation
Motto: "This problem will never be resolved."

The fourth and final pitfall on the path to reaching our full potential is the *scarcity mentality*. You'll know you've fallen into this trap when you hear yourself muttering self-defeating statements:

- "I'll never figure this out."
- "Nothing will ever change."
- "Life is just out to get me."
- "There's no use trying anymore . . ."

A truism often attributed to carmaker Henry Ford really *is* true: "Whether you believe you can do a thing or not, you are right."[5] Resigning yourself to a given problem forfeits the boundless fulfillment that comes from solving the problem. Please don't let that be you!

Several years ago, I chaired an organization called Opportunity International, which provides small-scale financial loans to entrepreneurs in need so they can begin to find release from the clutches of poverty. In the coastal city of Barranquilla, Colombia, a woman named Rosa fretted over her modest home. She fretted over her entire neighborhood, in fact, because it was situated on a landfill with no drainage system to speak of. Whenever heavy rains came—which they do with great frequency there—the water, having nowhere else to go, would rise up and flood her home.

Now, if anyone had cause for bellyaching or giving up, it was Rosa. Three times, she endeavored to raise the floor of her home to avoid future damage. Three times, her cobbled-together solution failed. Her situation was dire, and it worsened every time a storm rolled through town. Rosa could have resigned herself to the heavy weight of daily life, believing her load would never be lightened. Instead, she rallied. She found someone to teach her how to make soap. She learned how to purchase clothing for resale. She sought guidance regarding starting her own business. She got busy solving the next problem in front of her. And against all odds, she began to *thrive*.

Connecting with other homespun entrepreneurs caused her to cross paths with Opportunity International, which improved her situation even more when she was granted a roof-and-floor loan. By installing a permanent floor, Rosa ensured that her belongings would be safe, even in the midst of a storm. This mattered to her because those belongings included the handmade soap and articles of clothing that she sold out of her house. Not only is Rosa now proud of her home, but her business can also grow.

Regardless of how bad things may seem, change is only one solution away.

As is so often the case, taking action to change the order of things opens up further opportunities to change the order of things in bigger and better ways. What a testament to abundance thinking—to believing that, regardless of how bad things seem, change is only one solution away.

My guess is that you resonate most with one of these four pitfalls, that there's one that has caused you the most frustration in your effort to face and resolve problems in life. Take heart. In part 2, we will begin to hone the character qualities we need to navigate around these pitfalls on the path to realizing our full potential. To that end, it will be useful for you to have in mind two or three specific problems that are disrupting your world today. Though I still contend that problems are our friends, I concede that they can be *highly disruptive* friends.

Think back to when you were a kid learning to cross the street. I hope that some wise, wonderful adult pulled you aside and said, "Listen, you can't just barrel out into the street. The street is where cars drive. Cars can be dangerous. There is a *process* to crossing a street . . ."

No doubt that all-knowing person laid out for you a simple three-step approach to crossing a street: *stop*, *look*, *listen*. Those three steps can be covered in a matter of seconds, but those few seconds could save your life.

Stop, *look*, and *listen* was useful advice back then, and it's still useful for us today. As you endeavor to name the problems you'd like to solve, using the principles we'll discuss in part 2: "The Pursuit of the Path," I encourage you to try that simple trio again. Taking the time to stop, look, and listen is exactly the opposite of the termite's head-down approach: pushing dirt, day after day, never stopping to consider what may be all around.

First, *stop*. Your daily agenda and mine may look different, but I would venture a guess that we both lead busy lives. The simple act of stopping might be the most challenging thing you do all day. But it is a critical first step in analyzing what's really tripping you up. Stop. Sit. Breathe. Reflect. Find calm.

Next, *look*. Pick your head up and look around you. See things in a clear-eyed way. What is actually going on? What are the problems? Who else might be affected by these problems? The other people who live with you? Your colleagues at work? Are there systems you depend on to keep your days moving along? What's going on in your workplace, in your neighborhood, in your church, in your home? Is a friend going through a divorce? Is the school your kids attend losing people's trust? As you take in the various people and places that make up your typical week, what do you *see*?

Finally, *listen*. As you interact with other people in your life, what themes are you hearing? Is a family member hinting at a struggle he or she is walking through? Has a colleague consistently been making excuses for dropping the ball? Are your closest friends indicating that you've been tough to reach lately?

As you assess your present set of circumstances, what do you see? What do you hear? What problems are raising their hands in your life, hoping you'll choose them to solve? What thoughts are cluttering your mind, just waiting to get sorted out? What situations are making your life more difficult these days? Who seems bound and determined to give you heartburn lately? Consider jotting down the problems that are closest to you—those that surface in your mind and heart—so you'll have a list close at hand as you engage with the resources in part 2. By this point, I hope you're convinced that you don't want to be a termite, chained to a destination. I hope you're committed to solving problems with others, and staying on the path.

part two

THE PURSUIT OF THE PATH

chapter four

DECISIONS, DECISIONS

Your First,
Most Important Move

THIS IS WHERE the pushback invariably begins.

"But my problem is my boss . . . and I can't change my boss!"

"My problem is that I can't find work. I can't exactly *make* someone hire me."

"The biggest problem in my life is having too much month left at the end of the money. But my salary is what it is . . ."

The reasons for being stuck are plentiful: "*That* is why nothing will change."

To be fair, it is true that there are some things in life we simply cannot affect, which author David Richo calls the "givens of life." His list of five is lofty, but certainly correct:

1. Everything changes and ends.
2. Things do not always go according to plan.
3. Life is not always fair.
4. Pain is part of life.
5. People are not loving and loyal all the time.[1]

Perhaps a little more down to earth, I can also tell you that your boss is your boss. Your neighbors are your neighbors. The era you live in is pretty well fixed in time.

The past pains you've endured? Can't change those.

The heartbreak you've known? Can't change that.

Your DNA? Your height? Your shoe size? Your physical frame? Probably can't change these.

But just about everything else in life? Absolutely, positively fair game.

We can change our perspective. We can change our priorities. We can change our friends, our career, our outlook, our spending habits, our diet, our hair color, and whether we're an early bird, a night owl, or a lark. We can change where we live. We can change what we live *in*. We can change whom we live with.

I did not choose to get cancer. I could not change that I had cancer. But I could choose how to respond. I could change from being fearful to being grateful for the world-class care I received.

Yes, there are certainly things we cannot change in this life. But there are vastly more things that we can.

───

As I wrote in *Tough Choices*, the philosophy degree I earned had its roots in my fascination with Albert Camus and his 1942 work titled *The Stranger*. As a high schooler, I'd chosen that text (*L'Étranger*) for a French class project and had been drawn to the central theme of prioritizing *becoming* over *being*. As a child, I had dearly loved the words my mom had shared with my Sunday school class: "What you are is God's gift to you; what you make of yourself is your gift to God." Something about Camus's premise seemed to mesh with that sentiment.

We cannot choose who we are, I remember thinking as I read Camus, *but we can always choose to become something*

There are certainly things we cannot change in this life. But there are vastly more things that we can.

more. To stop choosing is to start dying. I desperately wanted to live.

As I dove headlong into higher education and then the workforce, I came to realize that 100 percent of leadership—both in life and in work—comes down to *choices.* Will I choose this city, or not? Take this job, or not? Befriend this person, or not? Attend this meeting, or not? Speak my mind, or not? Each decision, once made, leads to another set of choices, like branches sprawling from the trunk of a tree.

We cannot choose who we are, but we can always choose to become something more.

The realization sobered me—so much was riding on each individual choice! But I also found it exhilarating that each crossroads mattered so much. I became a student of my intentions, realizing that one decision, while seemingly inconsequential, could lead me either toward or away from the path I longed to be on. On this subject, author Gary Zukav has said that *intention* is the "why beneath the why."[2] I became keenly aware of my life's sequence of whys.

Years later, at the end of an interview I'd agreed to do, the reporter looked at me and said, "You are one of the most fiercely self-determined people I have ever met," a sentiment I received as a profound compliment. To determine oneself is to *define* oneself, which means that our *self* is not being defined by anything else—our circumstances, the opinions of others, or the expectations people have of us.

I must hold fast to that value, I thought after that interview. *I must always define myself.*

To define ourselves is to wield our true power, rather than giving it away to outside influences. Here in part 2, I will introduce a handful of practices—some individual, some collective—that will help keep your feet on the path that leads to your fullest potential. You can pursue these practices or abandon them. *Both options represent your choice.*

You may be tempted to cherry-pick the list: "Eh, I'm not much for collaboration—people are just so messy! But I'll give the courage thing a try."

You may be tempted to abdicate responsibility for the list: "Humility? Seriously? What world are you living in, Carly?"

You may be tempted to use the list to justify your misbehavior: "I would befriend the new hire, if only she weren't so rude . . ."

In light of these temptations, and perhaps others, allow me to plainly state two underlying truths:

You have more power than you realize.
You have probably given away that power more often than
  you realize.

I'll be the first to admit that the state of our world today is enough to make one want to curl up in a fetal position. Times are tough, and divisiveness is high. But it remains my contention that you and I are tougher. We are higher. *We are more powerful than we realize.*

The best research I can find on the topic of personal power says that only 10 percent of our fulfillment is based on external things, such as the quality of our relationships, the success we enjoy in our labors, the balance in our bank account, how popular we are.

> You have more power than you realize. You have probably given away that power more often than you realize.

Which means that a full 90 percent of our sense of satisfaction in life comes from intrinsic sources—that is, not our circumstances, *but how we respond to them*.[3] The way to get ourselves into trouble is to live as if our happiness depends on external factors.

"If only people would stop saying those things about me . . ."

"If only my boss could see the value I add . . ."

"If only I could afford *that* resource . . ."

"If only I'd had *those* opportunities . . ."

"If only I'd had that kind of time . . ."

"If . . . if . . . if . . ."

The downward spiral is easy to predict.

We strain and strive for outward success, for safety and security, for popularity and followers and likes. We give away our inherent power to those fleeting and fickle things. We wake up feeling powerless and lament our sorry state. We tank emotionally under the weight of our perceived impotence in a ravenously power-hungry world. We allow ourselves to be victimized by our circumstances and stalemates, our failures and foibles and fears. And we fail to realize that the only power these externals have is the power we choose to give them.

Demonstrating things like courage, character, and collaboration, the natural by-products of the practices I'll show you, will equip you to *take back the power you've given away*. These practices will reveal the choices you need to make to reclaim your power, multiply your power, and manage your power well over the long haul, as well as enabling you to pass on a powerful legacy to those you love. You are indeed powerful. Once you learn how to apply your massive strength, you'll know how to banish your deepest fears.

People close to me know that my Christian faith is important to me. As a person of faith, I believe you and I were created *on* purpose *for* a purpose, and that purpose centers on our solving the problems closest to us. It can be easy to move through life either ignoring the problems around you or else thinking, "Wow, that's a really big problem . . . somebody ought to solve that," without realizing that someone is *you*. Developing the ability both to *see problems* clearly and to *see yourself* as a possible solution to the problems closest to you is an important first step. However, I also need to make it clear that there is more to the story than just those two things.

It isn't enough to merely *see* the problem.

And it isn't even enough to *solve* the problem.

To reach your fullest potential, you must also understand that *how* you solve the problem is just as important as solving it.

During my days at AT&T, when I realized that becoming a problem solver was part of my pathway to success and impact, I also began to understand that as I solved external problems—matters dealing with organizational systems, with staffing dilemmas, with administrative odds and ends—I could simultaneously solve my internal issues as well. What were the fears that held me back? Where were the conflicts between my professed values and my actions? Why did I struggle in some relationships? What relational and organizational dynamics sapped my energy and made it difficult for me to hold on to hope? On and on the questions went. Fortunately, the answers weren't far behind.

As I looked around me, I saw many people who were defying their circumstances and having a real impact, right where they were. People like my mom and dad when I was growing up—a painter and a teacher, respectively, who didn't have fancy titles, highly visible roles, or the trappings of celebrity, yet who made their corner of the world a more life-giving place. I had teachers along the way who modeled teachability; managers who managed their power with great humility; colleagues who were collegial even when they could have isolated me or steamrolled me. I learned lessons from many different people and eventually arrived at a short but powerful list of highly desirable traits: *courage*, *character*, *collaboration*, and *creatively seeing possibilities*. Everybody I know who has been able to sustain their impact by addressing real problems, blessing others, and persevering over the long haul exemplifies these four key traits.

The more I saw these qualities put into practice by people I respected and admired, the more I realized that these specific practices, if adhered to, would keep me on the path toward my fullest potential. Further, I saw that embracing—or abandoning—these traits was 100 percent *my decision*. I could practice these things, or not. The choice was mine alone.

Courage is a choice. Character is a choice. Collaboration is a choice. Creatively seeing possibilities is a choice. These practices are all *intentional*—and I became determined to embrace them. I decided to focus on developing these practices, these empowering characteristics, instead of focusing on a destination I might never reach. I decided I would trust that the right opportunities would present themselves at the right time and in the right way.

My plea to you, as we examine these traits more closely in the next several chapters, is that *you* would make this choice. That you would decide to gather up your power and invest it wisely. That you would start now to develop and manifest the character qualities that will keep you on the path to your fullest potential. That you would focus on your intentions, motivations, and desires—the why beneath your why.

The path toward your full potential is the right path to be on, regardless of your personality type, your interests and aptitudes, or your life experiences. If you will commit to these practices and learn how to become a problem solver, you will realize your full potential. That is the earnest truth.

As we dive in together, another word of caution is in order. "Realizing your full potential" and "perfectly living out these traits" are two very different things. As it relates to courage and character, collaboration and creatively seeing possibilities, practice makes *imperfect*, and that's okay. Though many things lie within our control, there are some things we cannot change. We can't change other people, so if that's your goal, it's out. We can't change our physical stature, so if that's your goal, it's out. We can't change the past or the circumstances that find us day by day. These are a few of the things that make for an imperfect, sometimes bumpy ride. Multitalented Hollywood producer and pastor DeVon Franklin puts it succinctly: "The truth is, you and I are in control of only two things: how we *prepare* for what *might* happen, and how we *respond* to what *just* happened. The moment when things actually *do* happen belongs to God."[4] In other words, those moments when things actually happen? They're largely outside our control.

When I was a little girl, I joined the Brownies, which is the second- and third-grade division of the Girl Scouts. As part of our participation, we had to memorize the Girl Scout Law, which says, "I will do my best to be honest and fair, friendly and helpful, considerate and caring, courageous and strong, and responsible for what I say and do, and to respect myself and others, respect authority, use resources wisely, make the world a better place, and be a sister to every Girl Scout."[5] The beginning of that pledge was important to us girls: "I will do my best." Those five words really took the pressure off. Those five words said to me, "Things are going to happen. Mistakes will be made. Words will be said that can't be taken back. Lies will be told. Life won't be fair. But we can always strive to do our best."

What was true for me as a junior Girl Scout remains true today: We can do our best to value and apply key practices. We can uphold important character traits. We can get better at getting better, refusing to settle for who we are today, but always pressing on to who we can become. We can define ourselves by wise choices and priorities. We can pursue best practices, knowing they will move us forward on the path to becoming who we want to be. We can celebrate even the tiniest hints of courage and optimism—weren't all oak trees acorns to start? We can stay on the path we are meant to walk in this life, choosing each day to find our way.

chapter five

WHAT ARE YOU AFRAID OF?

The Courage to
Reclaim Your Power

SCOUR THE LANDSCAPE of phobias and you'll bump into some interesting fears. You've probably heard of arachnophobia (fear of spiders), ophidiophobia (fear of snakes), aerophobia (fear of flying), and acrophobia (fear of heights). But what about somniphobia (fear of sleep), ombrophobia (fear of rain), or haphephobia (fear of touch)?

Some people are afraid of being stuck in an elevator.

Others are afraid of putting their head underwater.

There are people who are afraid of thunder and lightning.

And some who are afraid of being alone.

If you and I were to chat long enough, we might add a few entries to the list. I know this because the experience of fear is part of being human. *Fearlessness* is a myth.

Recently, my Unlocking Potential team worked with some staff members from the Wounded Warrior Project, a veterans service organization that has provided both immediate comfort and long-term support to women and men injured in military battles since September 11, 2001. As our conversation unfolded, I realized that the heart of the issue was plain, old-fashioned *fear*. For example, the Project leaders went to great lengths to organize job fairs to help wounded veterans who needed a job connect with employers who were hiring. They would reserve a ballroom, order food and drink, and prepare accommodations for hundreds of attendees, but only ten or twelve people would show up. The lackluster turnout time and again was frustrating and discouraging for the organizers.

After hearing about this issue, I voiced the question that came to my mind: "What are they afraid of?" I figured if we could get to the bottom of the veterans' fear, we would understand why they stayed away and perhaps be able to make some helpful adjustments to the program.

The room fell silent for several seconds before a woman finally raised her hand and spoke.

"I myself am a wounded warrior," she said quietly, "and I know what they fear. They're afraid of coming to the job fair, talking to all these companies, and then not being offered the job. They're afraid of being pitied because of their injuries. They're afraid of failing. They're afraid of feeling worse than they already feel. They don't come to the job fair because they're *afraid* to come. It seems easier to just stay home."

I nodded my head in recognition. These folks who were staying home instead of pursuing the paycheck they so desperately needed were the same men and women who had come through enemy fire, jumped from helicopters, and sidestepped land mines. And *these* people were afraid.

To be human is to be afraid. Fearlessness is a myth.

My first experience with fear occurred when I was a very small child. Perhaps it was because I knew that both my parents had lost a parent, but I was desperately afraid I would lose them. I just knew that if I left their presence even for a moment, they would die. Or I would die. Or we all would die. I didn't know the term *thanatophobia* at the time, but I certainly suffered from the fear of death.

Most little girls love to have sleepovers with their friends, but never once did I go. Whenever my parents had to leave town for one reason or another, it was a major crisis in our home. My sister and brother would whoop and holler, thrilled that Mom and Dad would be gone for a few days, and I would fall mysteriously ill.

"Mommy, *please* don't go," I'd say. "I'm sick. You *can't* go now."

It didn't take long for Mom to figure out that her middle child was faking.

"I'm so sorry, but we have to go, honey," she'd say. And without fail, that declaration would break my heart. It got so bad that my parents could be going next door for a two-hour dinner party, and yet I would react as if I'd been orphaned. I would hole up in one of my siblings' rooms, lying in bed and reciting the Lord's Prayer over and over until they returned.

To be human is to be afraid. Fearlessness is a myth.

But what are we to do with our fear? How do we *live* when we're so afraid?

In one of those urban legends that make their way around the Internet from time to time, the story is told of a radio conversation between a US Navy ship and an unknown craft off the coast of Newfoundland. It was a foggy night, and every so often the ship's captain would notice a light flashing dead ahead through the mist. Assuming the beacon to be from a Canadian fishing boat, the captain got on the radio.

"Divert your course fifteen degrees north to avoid collision," he commanded.

A few seconds passed before a response crackled across the airwaves: "Divert *your* course fifteen degrees south to avoid collision."

Annoyed, the American captain radioed back: "I say again, divert your course fifteen degrees north."

Again, the laconic reply: "Divert your course fifteen degrees south."

The naval captain realized that unless something changed—and fast—a collision was inevitable. With tensions rising, he radioed, "This is the USS *Lincoln*, the second-largest ship in the United States' Atlantic fleet. We are accompanied by three destroyers, three cruisers, and numerous support vessels. I *demand* that you change your course fifteen degrees north—one-five degrees north—or countermeasures will be taken to ensure the safety of this ship!"

There was a brief pause, and then came this reply: "That's your call, Captain. This is a lighthouse."

Although the story has been debunked several times by Snopes and others—including the US Navy—the image of something immovable is useful for our purposes here. The fears we experience are like ships in the water: In due time, they will all pass. On the other hand, the strong and steady and secure lighthouse is like *courage*. It tells fear to alter *its* course, if only we'll stop allowing fear to hold so much sway.

After decades of battling fears in my own life—first of losing my parents, later of looking like a fool, among others—my firm belief is that fear has two possible destinies. The good news is that you and I get to *choose* which one will play out. Either fear will control us, consume us, and contain us, or we will control and contain *it*. Both cannot be true simultaneously, and only one of those outcomes serves us well. Either we lend power to *fear*—and stay locked up, shaky, afraid—or we lend power to *courage*, and thereby find the ability to thrive.

Back when I was a manager of engineering at AT&T, my team and I had to deal with one of our corporate attorneys who needed information from our group for one of his cases. He was a real piece of work. Whenever Glen the Lawyer called someone on my staff to make a request, instead of handling the exchange like a normal, civilized human being, he would yell and scream and often hang up on my team member. He was incredibly abusive, and I got quite an earful from my colleagues every time they received a call from Glen. One day, I'd finally had enough. I picked up the phone, dialed Glen's number, and told him, "You may not treat my team this way."

"Respect for the individual" was one of our core values at AT&T, and the members of my team were not being respected.

"Glen," I continued, "you need to be respectful of these people. They are working hard for you. They're jumping through all your hoops, in addition to doing their normal jobs. They deserve better than how you're treating them."

Glen the Lawyer was much higher in the organization than I was, which is perhaps why he wasn't too pleased with my telling him what he needed to do. I knew he wasn't happy because he expressed his displeasure right then and there, over the phone. In mostly four-letter words. He ended his verbal rampage with a question: "What are you going to do about it?"

It seemed I had stumbled upon a crossroads, and I knew I had a decision to make. *I can either lend power to courage*, I thought, *or else give power to my fear*.

"Glen," I said, "unless and until you apologize and behave differently, we will no longer do work for you."

With that, I hung up the phone. And then I burst into

tears. I may have lent power to courage on the outside, but inside I was a bundle of fear. After several moments of wondering what on earth I'd just done, I composed myself, walked out to where my team sat, and told them what I'd said to Glen. I instructed them not to do an ounce of work for him until further notice.

"I may have just gotten myself fired," I told them, "but I stand by what I've done. If you catch any heat from this, you make me the bad guy. Understood?"

Heads nodded and lips drew up into subtle grins. Nobody likes to be bullied. Nobody likes to be treated like scum. Glen the Lawyer had been put in his place, and even though my knees were knocking, I knew I had done the right thing.

It took Glen another two days before he fully got the message and called to apologize. But to his credit, he apologized to my team, and he apologized to me. Best of all, he made all future requests for information graciously, and my team was happy to comply.

I'd be remiss if I didn't fast-forward at this point to a more recent example of my needing to marshal a little courage in standing up to obnoxious behavior. This one occurred during the presidential debate season. In the fall of 2015, my team and I were on a cross-country blitz of key states, trying to entice voters to join our cause. One evening, I received a call from a young woman on my staff who was upset by something Donald Trump had said.

"What did he say now?" I asked, already weary of his conversational antics.

"It's about your face," she said.

She told me that the September issue of *Rolling Stone* magazine included a feature interview with Mr. Trump. During the interview with writer Paul Solotaroff, the two men evidently watched a newscast with Mr. Trump offering a running commentary. When a video clip zoomed in on me, Mr. Trump said, "*Look* at that face! Would anyone *vote* for that? Can you imagine that, the face of our next *president*?!"

When the others at the table, who had been laughing at his previous remarks, fell silent, he added, "I mean, she's a woman, and I'm not s'posedta say bad things, but really, folks, come on. Are we *serious*?"[1]

My campaign aide was almost in tears as she relayed the story to me, which is probably why she was shocked when she heard me laughing on the phone.

"How can you laugh about this?" she asked. "It's *terrible*."

I'll give her credit for being too young to know that women my age have spent an entire *lifetime* dealing with nonsense like this. Trump's remarks were merely the latest in a long, long line of comments made by men over the years about my appearance, my physique, or my gender—either positively or negatively—as a means of dismissing me altogether.

I told my staff to let it go, and I did the same.

Aside from answering a reporter's direct question regarding how I felt about the remark (I responded, "I didn't take the comments he made about me personally because he is an equal-opportunity insulter"), I didn't say anything about it. My second debate, with the full slate of Republican-ticket hopefuls, was a week away. I knew it would be addressed then. The only question remaining was, What would I say?

In advance of the debate, I focused on researching the policy issues I wanted to emphasize. I secured key stats and figures in my mind, and I finalized the points I wanted to ingrain in voters' minds. Despite my usual knack for planning ahead, I did not prepare a response for Mr. Trump.

"We'll just see what happens," I told my team.

During the debate, moderator Jake Tapper from CNN said he wanted to give Mr. Trump a chance to respond to a comment that fellow candidate Jeb Bush had made the previous week.

"Governor Bush told me last week when I read him the quote from [Louisiana] Governor Jindal that he agrees you're not a serious candidate," Jake began. "Tell Governor Bush why you are a serious candidate and what your qualifications are to be commander-in-chief."

Part of Mr. Trump's reply included the statement, "I heard what he had to say," delivered with mock offense. When I heard that line, I tucked it away. I knew I would be using it soon.

Later, when Jake Tapper asked me if I cared to respond to Mr. Trump's comments about my face, I said, "You know, it's interesting to me. Mr. Trump said that he heard Mr. Bush very clearly. . . . I think women all over this country heard very clearly what Mr. Trump said."

As the applause in the room died down, Mr. Trump leaned into his microphone and said, "I think she's got a beautiful face, and I think she's a beautiful woman."[2]

I stared straight ahead into the camera. Donald Trump's opinion of my face, beautiful or not, was his way of trying to diminish me. He never got the chance.

In the end, I was glad I hadn't practiced for the occasion. What "just happened" turned out to be perfect for the moment. By lending power to courage, saying only what needed to be said, and allowing Mr. Trump's words to form their own noose, I came out of that encounter with my dignity and my soul intact.

The point I want to make is this: By the time I found myself in a presidential debate, toe to toe on national television with someone who tried to dominate every exchange, I'd had so many opportunities to muster courage and tamp down fear that I wasn't the least bit afraid.

I know it sounds too good to be true, but *all* fear, no matter its consequence, can be contained. We don't have to be contained by it. Mark Twain once wrote that "courage is resistance to fear, mastery of fear—not absence of fear."[3] We cannot erase fear's presence from the course of our lives, but we can definitely put up a fight.

If you've ever had the experience of getting an MRI, you know what a terrible experience it is. You're asked to dress in a hospital gown, lie down on a conveyor belt, and place your body inside a fixed cage.

"Don't move," the technician reminds you. "Whatever you do, for the entirety of this test, don't move."

The technician then goes into a different room to watch you through a plate glass window as the conveyor belt moves you into an enclosed tube. If you weren't claustrophobic before, you are now. Through a microphone, the technician makes sure you're "all set," and then the imaging begins.

I don't know why the inventors of the MRI machine couldn't have made the sound of all those images being taken something like waves lapping against the shore or birds singing their morning songs, but they didn't. What they opted for instead was a jackhammer—a loud, persistent, mind-rattling jackhammer. By the time you come out, you can add *migraines* to whatever list of ailments had you receiving an MRI in the first place.

The situation couldn't get any worse, right? You're sick. You're stuck. There's a figurative jackhammer chiseling into your skull. Now, imagine that once you've been rolled into the tube and placed in position, you notice something strapped to the top of the machine, just inches above your head. Upon closer inspection, you discover that it's a live, three-foot-long snake on a box attached to the top of the scanner.

"Don't move," you hear the technician say again. "I'll need to ask you to remain completely still."

I wish I could tell you that this scene was fictional, but it's not. Two Israeli scientists who were conducting an experiment on fear attached a snake to the inside of an MRI machine and waited as unsuspecting patients were rolled into place. Then they collected brain-scan data to see what they could learn.

The results, I think, are fascinating. It turns out that when faced with a fearsome situation, the human brain experiences fear on two distinct levels. There is the fear you register as a threat to your body, and there is fear that you merely *feel*. One is objective—a snake is about to land on my face! And one is subjective—if I don't get out of here, I will surely die! The only time that fear cannot be contained is when we cave in to both types of fear at the same time.

To change the order of things, we must take action—bold, decisive action. Things don't get changed on their own.

A reporter for *Scientific American* said of the experiment's findings,

> You could say that you are not afraid but sweat a lot, or say that you are freaked out and sweat not at all. But here is the interesting thing: as long as these two disagree, you would act courageously. It is only when you scored high on both, sweat and fear, that you would succumb to cowardice. It is as if you have two brakes. Release either one, and you could drive on.[4]

It's normal to feel anxiety when we decide to face fear. But sometimes we simply have to tell ourselves, "Don't freak out."

To reach your fullest potential and live the life of impact for which you were made, you will have to marshal great courage—perhaps more often than you realize. Think about it: The path to your fullest potential is paved with problems, problems *you* are intended to solve. But to solve those problems, you must work to change the order of things. Something is wrong that must be set right. A system is broken, a relationship is fractured, someone is being mistreated, a value isn't being upheld.

To change the order of things, you must *take action*—bold, decisive action. After all, things don't get changed on their own.

To take bold, decisive action is to subject yourself to criticism. And who in their right mind wants *that*?

The reason problems stick around for so long, festering

until they stink, is not that people don't see them. Everyone *sees* the problems! Though some people want change to happen, those who are invested in the status quo may want things to stay the way they are. So change is always difficult. One reason those problems don't get solved sooner is that nobody wants to be criticized for making the changes that need to be made.

When I left my role as CEO of Hewlett-Packard, I left with my honor intact. During my six years there, my colleagues and I had made significant changes and solved substantial problems. I was, and am, extremely proud of what we accomplished, and yet to read the news stories that came out in the days following my departure, you'd have thought I was evil incarnate—or worse. I was "too flashy." I was "vindictive." Employees had "never liked me." I don't know how such treatment would have affected you, but it was hard for me to swallow. I'm a recovering people-pleaser. I care *deeply* about what people think. I want to be accepted and liked and valued and esteemed, and yet here I was being portrayed as an utter failure—and in front of the entire world, no less! And yet what was I supposed to do? I could hand over my power to the fears that tried to crop up—that everyone hated me, that I had embarrassed myself, that I would never amount to anything again—or I could take a different tack and stand my ground.

The facts were these: When I realized that two of our board members were leaking sensitive corporate information to the press, I told the entire board that the situation was intolerable to me. Either we had to put a stop to the leaks and ensure they never happened again—it was a clear violation of our code of conduct—or I would leave. Though we all knew the sources of the leaks, no one would ever own up. Another board member encouraged me on several occasions to "let it go."

I *couldn't* let it go.

Later, when it became clear to me that the rest of the board wasn't prepared to take action against these two board members and too many were prepared to let me go instead, I could have chosen to tie up the proceedings for months, exercising my right as a board member to vote against my own firing.

I wouldn't cast that vote.

By a majority of one, then, the board voted to kick me out.

Hours later, their outside counsel approached me with the news that the board wanted me to paint my departure as my own decision—that I had accomplished all I'd set out to accomplish and I was ready to move on to other challenges.

I did not agree to that plan.

Had I caved to all my old fears, I would have behaved far differently than I did. But courage called me to a strength I didn't know I had. I stood firmly on my values. I accepted my departure. And I insisted on telling the truth. I wouldn't change a thing.

On the heels of my abrupt dismissal, friends called in tears of outrage and disgust. "How could they *do* this to you, Carly? How on earth are you *handling* all of this?"

To be clear, I was not happy about what happened. In fact, for the next three years, I couldn't even drive by HP headquarters because it churned my stomach so much. But all the drama? All the pretense? All the outrage and disgust?

I was glad to have it behind me. I was at peace with what had happened. I had made my own choices, and I could live with them. I could tell the truth, and I was proud of my record.

The truth was, I had (and still have) a very happy marriage. I loved being home for once. I lived in a beautiful place, and in freedom. What right did I have to complain?

I guess I'd put it like this: I wanted to preserve my happiness and my integrity more than I wanted to even the score. Because I could live with my choices, I moved forward.

Meanwhile at HP, the board—like many dysfunctional teams—thought that if they got rid of the people who were focused on the problem, they would get rid of the problem itself. But after I was gone, and several other board members resigned, the problems continued to grow because the board never truly confronted the dysfunction that was the root cause of the leaks. Ultimately, the problems consumed the board, and the acrimony burst into public view. Eighteen months after my dismissal, the two leakers were fired from the board, the new chairman was forced to resign, and the company was subjected to congressional hearings.

My first public appearance following my unceremonious departure from HP was a commencement speech at North Carolina A&T. I remember looking out at the sea of fresh college grads and thinking, *We have so much in common, you and I.*

I told the graduates that when I'd first received the invitation to speak to them, I was the CEO of an $80 billion company with 145,000 employees in 178 countries around the world. But after my untimely exit and the blistering news reports, I'd called the chancellor to see if he still wanted me to speak.

Graciously, he'd said, "Carly, if anything, you can probably relate to these students even better now than you could before."

He couldn't have been more correct. Like those recent graduates, I'd been working on my résumé. Like those graduates, I'd been lining up my references. Like those graduates, I'd bought a new interview suit. And like those graduates, if any recruiters happened to be in the audience, I was more than happy to talk.

What benefit will it be to you if you gain the whole world but lose your soul?

That part of my talk sparked genuine laughter from the audience and genuine growth in me. Simply showing up that day confirmed a deep-seated choice I hope I will always make: *I will not let fear rule my life.*

I ended my speech by saying, "I am at peace and my soul is intact. I could have given it away and the story would be different. But I heard the word of Scripture in my head: 'What benefit will it be to you if you gain the whole world but lose your soul?'"[5]

The sustained applause from the audience overwhelmed me and lifted me up.

Now, to *your* situation. To the problems *you* are meant to solve. How will you overcome the fears that tie you up in knots, to unlock the potential that's there inside? To help you

WHAT ARE YOU AFRAID OF?

sort out your answer and put fear in its rightful place, let me give you a three-pronged place to start:

1. Name your fear.
2. Run toward it.
3. Take your power back.

As silly as it may sound, the simple act of telling the engineers at AT&T that I was afraid my conversation with Glen the Lawyer would cost me my job helped me wrap my arms around what was really behind my anxious thoughts and sweaty palms. That job meant a lot to me, and the thought of losing it—and perhaps sidetracking my entire career—was terrifying to me. Interestingly, as the words came out of my mouth—"I may have just gotten myself fired"—a rush of power came flowing in. Can something as straightforward as naming our fears kick-start the process of stripping them of the power they hold over us? My heartfelt answer is *yes*. I know it, because I've lived it. I've seen firsthand what *naming fears* can do.

Give it a try. I dare you.

What is it that you're afraid of? What fears are tripping you up today?

Maybe you're afraid of being pitied, like those Wounded Warriors were.

Maybe you fear being marginalized for admitting who you really are.

Are you afraid you're never going to get married, or that you'll never become a mom?

Are you afraid you'll lose a job you love and not get the chance to really soar?

Are you afraid of what "they" think of you? Do their opinions haunt your thoughts?

Are you afraid of disappointing your loved ones by not doing what they think you should do?

Are you afraid you won't hit the deadline that's closing in on you?

Are you afraid you'll look like a fool?

Are you afraid you'll never get beyond a troubled relationship?

Are you afraid your life won't amount to much?

Are you afraid that disease will take your life?

That your addiction will have its way?

Are you afraid you'll never be able to make ends meet?

Or that by trying something new, you'll fail?

When I chaired the board for the nonprofit Opportunity International, after a board meeting in New Delhi, India, I wanted to meet some of the women to whom our organization had issued microfinance loans of roughly one hundred dollars each. As my team and I made our way across town, the sights and sounds overwhelmed me. Piles of trash created their own topography. Hungry feral animals marauded through the streets. People sandwiched themselves one atop another, having no other place to go. The scene was grim, and I remember steeling myself as I climbed the makeshift ladder to the appointed meeting place, a primitive rooftop seating area above one of the women's homes.

I reached the top rung of the ladder and saw the faces of the women I was there to meet. I did not see desperation. Instead I saw pride, hope, determination. These women were not brooding; they were *beaming*. These were women who had faced fear and won.

I asked one of the women to tell me her story.

She told me that she hailed from an ultra-traditional part of India, where strict cultural norms dictate that women are not to be taught or trained.

"It is a waste of effort," she explained. "That's what our culture thinks."

You can imagine, then, that when the opportunity came for her to receive a loan from Opportunity International, her parents and husband and in-laws all insisted that she decline. This woman knew that taking the loan would compromise her relationship with everyone she held dear, but the alternative was equally disturbing: a lifetime of poverty with no way out.

"It took me one year to decide," she said, "but eventually, I took the loan." A full year to screw up her courage—can you imagine? And yet she finally, and decisively, showed up for herself. Day by day, she rattled off her fears, weakening their hold on her a little each time.

I'm afraid of going against my culture.
I'm afraid of refusing my family's advice.
I'm afraid of what people will say about me.
I'm afraid of being marginalized or disowned.
I'm afraid of all this and more.

But do you know what fear finally eclipsed all the rest? The fear of never knowing if she could have won out over them.

"What does your family think about you taking that loan now?" I asked.

"Now? Oh, they are very happy now. They all work for me today."

To put your fears in their rightful place, first identify them by name.

I'm afraid of failing.
I'm afraid of not trying.
I'm afraid of looking stupid.
I'm afraid of not fitting in.
I'm afraid of letting down someone I love.

Name the fear. Literally, say it aloud. Bonus points if you name it in the presence of another person. And then, before moving on, sit for a moment with the words you've declared.

After you've named your fear, *run toward it*. Relax. It's not as scary as it sounds.

If I have learned anything about fear along the way, it's this: The more we practice displaying courage, the more predictably we will move past the anxiety that weighs us down. Running toward our fear is like running at the gym; the more we do it, the more natural it becomes. Notice I didn't say, the *easier* it becomes. The truth is, it may never get easier. It will, however, become more predictable; you will know what to expect.

If you're like me, you never really *feel* like going to the gym—even though you know how amazing and strong you'll feel afterward. You can find a million and one ways to get out of a workout: It's too hot, it's too cold, you're too busy, you're too tired, you're too hungry, you're too full, traffic is a nightmare, the stars in the sky aren't aligned. And yet as soon as you set foot on that treadmill, you're glad you came. Yes, it's gonna hurt. Yes, your body is going to revolt. Yes, you'll dream up sixteen different ways to cut your run a little short and head home. But if you can just push past those gremlins that taunt you, if you can persevere for just a mile or so, the workout will take care of itself. You'll be *in*, no turning back.

Courage is a lot like getting in shape, I think. Is it painful to face our fears? It is. Would it be easier to stay home and keep our heads down? It would. But if we summon even an ounce of courage, that momentum can carry us forward. The reason I was able to display courage in the face of Glen the Lawyer's bullying was that it wasn't the first time I'd faced down fear. In that same organization, when I was a lowly salesperson still cutting her teeth, I was assigned to a crotchety man named Carl, who had been in sales longer than I'd been alive. He was horrified to be paired with me, and he made it known it in some not-so-subtle ways.

Case in point: For the first client meeting I was to be involved in, Carl came over to my desk to inform me that the client had picked the meeting place.

"We'll be going to The Board Room," he said. And as he turned to leave, he added with a smirk, "I guess you won't be joining us after all."

Moments later, I learned from a colleague that The Board Room was a strip joint in downtown DC, where local businessmen often lunched. This was Carl's way of shutting me out of the deal. I knew it; he knew it; and the client knew it as well. I went and hid in the ladies' room.

I cried tears of rage. It was so unfair!

I prayed.

What was I supposed to do here? Which way was I supposed to go?

Taking my own advice, I named my fear: "I don't want to look like a fool."

Incidentally, this was a reasonable fear to have. In those days, I dressed according to John T. Molloy's 1977 bestseller, *The Woman's Dress for Success Book*, which included detailed instruction on how to tie a bow tie, of all things. As luck would have it, not only was I wearing a very conservative suit that day, but I also had on *a striped bow tie*.

There on the cold tile of the bathroom, as I sat with how I was feeling, I realized there was a fear that went deeper than my fear of looking foolish—namely, the fear that I would not be able to do my job. As soon as that realization hit me, I made a decision in my heart: I would go to the strip club with Carl. I would show what I was made of. I would not let fear win.

So I went. When I told the cab driver where I was going, dressed as I was with my bow tie and briefcase, he turned around in his seat and asked, "So, are you the new act?"

This was not starting out well.

I entered the strip club, paused for a moment to allow my eyes to adjust to the dim interior lighting, and searched the crowd for Carl. As luck would have it, the place was packed that afternoon, which meant I had to work my way along the edge of a bar that filled one side of the club. Across from the bar, on a giant stage, there was a live act going on. The dozens of patrons seated around tables—all upstanding businessmen, of course—must have wondered what turnip truck I had fallen off of as I went from one corner of the restaurant to the other. But eventually, I made it to the client's table—briefcase, bow tie, and all.

It was as horrifying an experience as it sounds, and yet I don't regret it. For one thing, I made it out alive. But more important, Carl began treating me as a peer the very next day.

My point is this: If we can keep showing up, keep challenging our fears, keep pressing into the power we already possess, these fights will eventually be won. We'll keep making it out alive.

I probably don't seem like the type to follow the "sport" of bullfighting—and I'm not—but I remember coming across a concept from that realm that has stayed with me to this day.

Evidently, in bullfighting, there is a place within the ring where the bull will retreat when it is feeling highly threatened. At first, the bull will engage with the bullfighter—the *torero*—in the ring, but as barbed sticks are thrust into the bull's shoulders by the *picadors*, the bull feels increasingly afraid. And then that fear turns to rage. Agitated beyond what it can bear, the bull will charge off, away from the torero, to his *querencia*, his hiding place, where he will assume a defensive stance.

The first time or two that the bull races off to its querencia, the torero may not recognize what is happening. But soon enough, the fighter is onto the bull.

"Ah, that is where you go to hide!"

Once the torero understands the bull's pattern, he can beat him to the punch. He can send a picador to lie in wait in the bull's querencia, making it all but impossible for the bull to retreat and gain strength. The matador is then engaged, and the beleaguered bull charges and is subsequently put to death.

The proposition I'd like you to consider is that we all have our querencias. We have places where we retreat when we've had enough of being poked by fear. We retreat to isolation. Or busyness. We retreat to addictions, or depression, or sloth. We retreat to social media. We retreat to reality television. We retreat to online shopping. We retreat—so often!—to food. We go to a place where it feels safe. What we don't realize, however, is that we're sealing our own fate.

It is far better, before we are weakened and demoralized by the barbs of fear, to charge out from our querencias, directly toward whatever threatens to take us down. It is far better to face our fears with confidence—sweaty palms and knocking knees notwithstanding. It is far better to steady our stance, stand our ground, and remind ourselves not to freak out. Practice may not make perfect here, but it certainly makes things more predictable. And in terms of overcoming the slithering, beady-eyed fears that hover around our heads, that's good enough for me.

Name your fear. Run toward it. And prepare to take back your power.

Once you have spoken aloud the fear that strikes terror in your heart, grab a journal and a pen. It's time for a bit of introspection, a little truth-telling, just you and your soul.

As you name your fear and run toward it, I want you to answer two questions:

What is the worst that could happen here?

What is the best outcome imaginable?

Back when I was deliberating whether to go to the lunch at the strip club, I remember thinking, *Although it will surely embarrass me to walk in there, at least it will signal to Carl that I'm here to stay.*

Honestly? The trade-off was worth it. The worst thing that could happen, I figured, was humiliation, and that wasn't that scary to me. On the blessing side of the equation, the *best* thing that could happen was something I would only be able to see in hindsight, as I processed things later that night.

Part of what made The Board Room famous was that the women could be called over for table dances. While the men were enjoying their liquor-fueled lunches, dancers wearing see-through negligees would entertain them on the tabletop.

During our lunch that afternoon, Carl called over no fewer than three dancers to provide this added service. But on each occasion, upon seeing me sitting at the table, the dancer would say, "Not until the lady leaves."

I counted that little act of woman-to-woman solidarity as a blessing that day.

Of far greater consequence was a fear I once faced regarding Frank's and my daughter Lori. I wrote extensively about Lori's life and her untimely death in my book *Rising to the Challenge*, so I won't repeat the details here. But I will say that when you lose a child to addiction, you feel a certain sense of shame. A cloud hovers over your head and follows you everywhere.

Wasn't there something I could have done?

Even as I know deep in my bones that only the addict can stop an addiction, the grief over losing Lori was utterly unbearable at times.

For many months, I avoided discussion of our loss with friends, colleagues, and coaching audiences alike. What could I say? What would they think? Truthfully, the latter of those two concerns was the one that kept me silent, stifled by fear. I was terrified that speaking of Lori's death would paint me in a negative light. My daughter was an *addict*? She *died* from her addiction? There was *nothing* I could do? But over time, I realized that the only way to free myself from fear was to practice *courage*, one step at a time. That's true for everyone who is hemmed in by fear.

What's the worst thing that could happen? I asked myself.

I couldn't think of a single thing.

I gradually began talking about how I felt about Lori's death, about her absence, and about her pain. I opened up with family, and then with friends, and then with clients. I'll never forget the day I told an entire audience about Lori— her struggle, her beauty, her life. Following my talk, a woman from the audience approached me and said, "*Thank you* for sharing what you did about your daughter. I'm in the very same situation, and you can't imagine my relief over knowing I'm not alone."

Someone will thank me. I hadn't thought to put that on my best-thing-that-could-happen list, but there it was.

If you have spent a lifetime (or even an hour) allowing fear to rule your world, I have good news for you. No matter how long it has been since you lost your way, you can find it again, starting right now. By letting courage seep into your ways, you can choose to reclaim the power you've been giving away. Even if you've never done it before, you can practice being brave. This is the first and most important choice you will ever make. All other decisions you make to take back your power flow from here.

Psychologist Rebecca Ray has a great way of putting this idea. "It's okay to be scared," she writes in her book *Be Happy*. "Doing something that's unfamiliar, like giving yourself permission to heal, or following your dreams, or being raw and vulnerable, takes courage. And courage only shows up when fear is present first."[6]

Do you see? Fear is necessary in our lives because it cues us to let courage in. We know it's time to summon our strength when weakness is at the front door.

As you display courage in your own life, you'll bring strength to many others. Courage loves company.

But I have even better news: As you display courage in your own life, you'll bring strength to many others beyond yourself. Want to know Dr. Ray's professional philosophy? "Courage loves company." Frankly, I couldn't agree more. My mind flashes to the recent story involving an ill-intentioned sports-medicine doctor, Larry Nassar, and scores of USA gymnasts—just *girls*, really . . . third graders, some of them. Officially, Dr. Nassar was accused of molesting more than

250 young women (and one young man) but admitted to only ten of those accusations. In the Michigan courtroom in January 2018, you would have been hard-pressed to find anyone who was sympathetic to innocence on *any* count, as more than 150 women stepped to the podium microphone to detail the abuses they'd faced.

One of those spokeswomen was two-time Olympic medalist Aly Raisman, who captained the United States Olympic gymnastics team in 2012 and 2016. She looked strong as she delivered her remarks to Mr. Nassar, who was seated just ten feet away.

"Imagine feeling like you have no power and no voice," she said. "Well, you know what, Larry? I have both power and voice, and I am only just beginning to use them. All these brave women have power, and we will use our voices to make sure you get what you deserve: a life of suffering spent replaying the words delivered by this powerful army of survivors."[7]

Ms. Raisman later told reporters that she hadn't planned to speak in court. "I was scared and nervous," she said—but she chose to follow through once she heard the impact statements other victims had delivered.[8] Courage loves company—do you agree? When one of us steps up to do the right thing, others are emboldened to follow suit.

chapter six

WHO YOU ARE WHEN NO ONE'S LOOKING

Multiplying Your Power for Good

We don't use the term *character* much anymore in our society, but during my growing-up years it was common to hear people talk about it, and everyone knew what it meant.

"Character is about candor," my dad always told my siblings and me. "It's about integrity, and about standing up for what you believe. It's about consistency with these things over time."

My sister, my brother, and I would dutifully nod our heads, though we barely grasped all that those words entailed. But over time, as it so often does, our understanding grew. We began to see what Dad was talking about, what character looked like in people, and why we should care.

Character, though sometimes cumbersome to define with words, is clear when we observe it in someone's life. It's one thing to declare our beliefs and values, but it's quite another thing to stand up for those values day after day before the world, when under pressure, attack, scrutiny, or criticism.

It's one thing to admit we've made a mistake, but quite another to stick around to make things right.

It's one thing to acknowledge that there's a problem, but quite another to raise our hands to solve it.

What, then, is that "quite another thing"? It is integrity, courage, and honor displayed consistently over time.

Think for a moment about a time when you've seen someone manifest strength of character. What were the dynamics involved? How did he or she respond?

I spent the majority of 2009 battling breast cancer, and I met plenty of people involved in that same fight who displayed great strength of character. Despite the pain, uncertainty, and disillusionment that accompany that disease, these people did not give in to despair. They showed up, with hope alive in their hearts and words of encouragement on their lips, determined to finish strong, regardless of the outcome. Their strength of character—their determination to keep moving forward—had a profound effect on me. It made it easier for me to be hopeful, encouraging, and determined.

If you're a baby boomer like me, then your parents lived through the Great Depression of the 1930s, the longest, most widespread economic downturn in American history. Examples abound from that era of women and men who refused to give in, refused to give up, believing instead that brighter days would soon dawn. That daily decision to choose integrity, perseverance, and hope yielded a legacy of strong character, which is why that group has been dubbed "the greatest generation."

I think of my late friend Senator John McCain as a man of character. He was serving his country in 1967 during the Vietnam War when the unthinkable happened. On his twenty-third bombing mission over North Vietnam, John's plane was shot down by a missile, and he was subsequently captured by Vietnamese forces. The ejection from his aircraft broke both of John's arms and one of his legs, and after he landed in a lake in the city of Hanoi, he nearly drowned. He was pulled ashore by Viet Cong soldiers, who crushed John's shoulder with the butt of a gun before transporting him to a holding bin for prisoners of war. There, he was interrogated, beaten, and denied medical treatment for his injuries. He lost fifty pounds during that ordeal, but he never lost his will to live. Those in charge of the prison, the so-called Hanoi Hilton, tried to force John to sign a confession that they planned to use as war propaganda, but he gave them nothing they could use. He was beaten three or four times a week for denying their request.[1] Real integrity. Proven over time. By a man of character.

Civil-rights activists who practice peaceful protest over a period of not weeks or months, but years, understand strength of character. As do career first responders. And parents of children with special needs. And families hamstrung by poverty of one kind or another. We see their faces and read their stories and marvel at their way of life. We ask ourselves, "How on earth do they handle that challenge?"

They choose integrity, courage, and honor.

Over a long period of time.

On purpose and *for* a purpose beyond themselves.

That's how they handle it.

———

As I mentioned in a previous chapter, I became fascinated early in my career by the qualities that distinguish people with great impact from those without. *Character* is one of those traits. Why is character necessary? How does one pursue it? What can a character-based person expect in life?

What came from those years of observation are four essential truths about character.

1. Character is critical when the going gets tough. (And the going always gets tough.)

As I was considering the role of CEO at HP, I initiated dozens of conversations with the board of directors, in an attempt to clarify as many things as possible before I said yes. I wanted to do my due diligence and then some. I wanted to know fully what I was getting myself into, to be confident that the board and I saw the situation in the same way.

HP was founded by two college buddies from Stanford, Bill Hewlett and Dave Packard, who were both electrical engineering majors. The story of how they started the company in a one-car garage in Palo Alto during the Great Depression with only an initial investment of five hundred bucks and a vision to change the world was a deeply ingrained part of company lore, as well as Silicon Valley history.

Over time, Bill and Dave crystallized their approach to business into five tenets that became known as the HP Way: We have trust and respect for individuals; we focus on a high level of achievement and contribution; we conduct our business with uncompromising integrity; we achieve our common objectives through teamwork; and we encourage flexibility and innovation.[2] These are wonderful values that spawned a powerful culture. Over time, however, the phrase "the HP Way" became more important than the substance behind it. Too often, the HP Way became shorthand for "that's the way we've always done it and that's how it's going to stay." The HP Way became not a clarion call for innovation, but a shield against change. Predictably, perhaps, those who had known Bill and Dave—or, in some cases, were *related* to Bill and Dave—became fierce guardians of tradition, even when that tradition had long since become counterproductive. The HP board was aware that the family members who joined the board after Bill and Dave left the company were a potential problem. But they assured me many times that these family members would not be a factor.

But wouldn't you know it, on day two of my tenure at HP, a family member showed up in my office with an announcement to make.

"As you know," he said, "the board asked me to resign. But I'm sure you're going to change the decision." Which I did not.

Thus began my experience with members of the founders' families, a saga that continued long after they really were "not a factor."

One thing I've learned is that a certain amount of turmoil is par for the course. In my experience, nothing meaningful, nothing lasting, nothing of substance comes about without something of a fight, because change is always hard. The way things have always been has great power. Tough times demand great character from us; and the times *always* get tough.

Business psychologist Susan David, creator of the "emotional agility" concept, once spoke about life's audacity to be tougher than we planned.

I've had hundreds of people tell me what they don't want to feel. They say things like "I don't want to try because I don't want to feel disappointed." Or "I just want this feeling to go away."

"I understand," I say to them. "But you have dead people's goals. Only dead people never get . . . inconvenienced by their feelings. Only dead people never get stressed, never get broken hearts, never experience the disappointment that comes with failure."

Tough emotions are part of our contract with life. You don't get to have a meaningful career or raise a family or leave the world a better place without stress and discomfort. Discomfort is the price of admission to a meaningful life.[3]

Dr. David couldn't be more correct. Once we dive into the task of solving meaningful problems, we realize that things will never be as smooth or straightforward as we imagined them to be—despite even the most careful planning. It won't be as fun. It won't be as exciting. It won't be as victorious as we dreamed. Which is why long-term courage is required. It's not just that we're getting the ball rolling; most times, it's that we're rolling the ball *uphill*.

To have a positive impact, then—to make a positive contribution on any significant level—we must display strength of character. Even when we don't want to. Even when nobody else is doing it. Even when it's hard. Perhaps especially when it's hard. Character is the recognition that when the going gets tough—and it always does—we persevere. We don't look for shortcuts. We muster persistence and tenacity, and we forge ahead.

2. Contrary to popular opinion, the ends never justify the means.

In the corporate world, an insane amount of pressure congregates around an exercise known as "hitting the quarterly numbers." "The numbers" refers to a company's revenues or profits or new customers over a three-month period, relative to the quarterly projections made by the leaders of the organization. The numbers are a big deal in every public company because they are a big deal to Wall Street, shareholders, and competitors.

> *Character is the recognition that when the going gets tough—and it always does— we persevere. We don't look for shortcuts.*

As I've said on many occasions, hitting the numbers is the easiest thing in the world to do. A shift in the balance sheet here, some creative orchestration there, and voilà, the numbers get hit. The issue is always *how* the numbers get hit. One complicating factor is a little thing called *ethics*. As in, doing what's right every time, whether anyone's watching or not.

On one occasion when I was coming up the ranks in corporate life, I remember working late on New Year's Eve, trying to finalize a big contract with a client. At the time, the organization's fiscal year ran according to the calendar year, and I knew that if the next day dawned and I didn't have this signed contract in hand, we would miss our numbers. By a lot. Still, there was only so much I could do, and in the end, it wasn't enough.

On New Year's morning, I made the call I did not want to make. My boss picked up the phone, I explained what had happened, and then my heart sank low in my chest as I listened to his response.

"Can't you just predate the contract?" he said, less a question than a direct command.

I sat in stunned silence.

"Carly?" he said. "Did you hear me? This is an easy fix, you know . . ."

So much was riding on our quarterly numbers, not the least of which was the size of my boss's bonus. I exhaled audibly, praying for courage I did not feel, and said, "That's not something I'm willing to do."

We missed the quarter, and my boss was enraged. Still, I slept well those nights.

Later, when I was CEO at HP and we were trudging through the economic recession of the early 2000s, I was approached by an executive with a "suggestion." The outlook for that quarter-end wasn't good, a fact I knew well.

"There's the warehouse option," the executive said, assuming I knew what he meant. He went on to explain that one of our warehouses held a significant amount of HP equipment on one side and equipment belonging to one of our customers on the other. As such, there were two balance sheets in play in that warehouse—the customer's and ours. If we simply instructed the warehouse personnel to scoot some of our equipment to the other side of the room, in other words, we could hit our numbers with ease.

This was clearly not ethical. Perhaps no one on the outside would know, but *we* would know. *I* would know. We shut this down and made sure that everyone understood we would never, ever make the numbers this way.

A significant aspect of character development is understanding the difference between short-term and long-term gain. No doubt, had I signed my name to "the warehouse option," our stakeholders and the brokers on Wall Street would have cheered. But what would I have gained in the end, in terms of respect from my senior-most team? I would have proved that I would do *anything* to get the immediate-term monkey off my back. It would have sent a message to my team that it was okay to cut corners—and it would have made it easier for us to cut the next corner. That's a slippery slope. Today, it's the warehouse option; tomorrow, it's . . .

Let's face it: Sometimes it can be very tempting in the short term to cut those corners, to do what's necessary—though maybe not right—to achieve an end. But in the long run, it never pays off. The ends never justify the means, especially when the means are dishonest.

Had I followed through with either of these shifty plans, I would have done what author and cultural commentator David Brooks calls *putting our loves out of order*. He writes,

> We all have a sense that some loves are higher or more important than other loves. I suspect we all rank those loves in pretty much the same way. We all know that the love you feel for your children or parents should be higher than the love you have for money. We all know the love you have for the truth should be higher than the love you have for popularity. Even in this age of relativism and pluralism, the moral hierarchy of the heart is one thing we generally share, at least most of the time.
>
> But we often put our loves out of order. If someone tells you something in confidence and then you blab it as good gossip at a dinner party, you are

putting your love of popularity above your love of friendship. If you talk more at a meeting than you listen, you may be putting your ardor to outshine above learning and companionship.[4]

Regardless of my finance team's justifications—which were myriad—if we had manufactured inflated earnings so that some business analysts and investors would be pleased, it was more than a little likely that we were putting our love for praise and a short-term bump in the stock price well above our love for the truth and long-term achievement.

I know this position is not always obvious when you observe the behavior of many politicians or executives in business, in sports, in religion, or in the media, but "victory at any cost"—whether referring to financial figures, polling numbers, or anything else—violates the heartbeat of character. It's not just the win that matters, but also *how* you win. My mom used to say, "Carly, the mills of God grind exceedingly slow, but they grind exceedingly fine." The practice of character may not yield immediate, socially approved benefits, but it certainly yields strength for the soul.

When we forsake immediate gain—the acceptance, the accolades, the yes vote, the win—in favor of long-term benefit, we carve out a deeper capacity for good things such as *honor* and *integrity* to take hold. We order our heart's affections in a manner that aligns more closely with the type of people we want to become.

No doubt you've heard the saying "Tough times build character." I think it's more accurate, perhaps, to say, "Tough times *reveal* character." How we choose to respond when the going gets tough reveals who we are. Likewise, how we choose to behave when the stakes are high and the end goal is important—when no one is looking and we don't think anyone will ever find out—reveals who we truly are. Character is who we choose to be over the long haul, under pressure, and when no one is looking.

Don't become corrupted by the system, no matter how corrosive it may be. Don't become so down and dirty out there that you forget what it feels like to be clean. Consider others' needs above your own. Amid all the violence and vanity and dishonesty and deceit in the world, never forget the loveliness and joy and peace that accompany a life lived with integrity. Whatever you need to do to stay in touch with integrity, commit to those things. Build a faith worth keeping and keep the faith. And this: Tell yourself the truth.

I have found it useful to ask myself a few questions from time to time:

Do I always do the right thing, even when no one is looking?

Is the Carly that people see the same as the Carly when nobody's watching?

Are all my loves in order?

If the answer to these is *yes*, then I know I'm free—free to anticipate what lies ahead, with no fear whatsoever about "being found out" or "getting caught." I'm free to release my concern about what people might think if they knew the real me. Why? Because the real me is what they already see. My public and private selves are integrated.

And the best news? This freedom isn't reserved for anyone special; it's available to all of us. Integrity is the key.

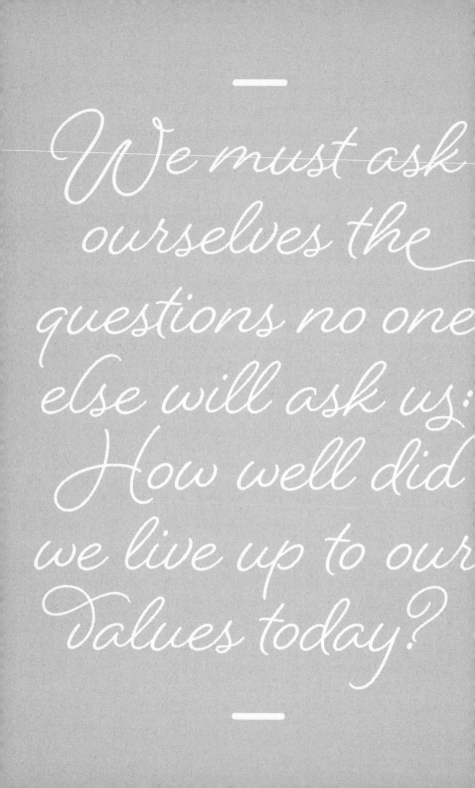

We must ask ourselves the questions no one else will ask us: How well did we live up to our values today?

3. Character demands reflection, and reflection can't be rushed.

Motivational speaker and entrepreneur Jim Rohn built a veritable self-help empire in the last third of the twentieth century. He was known for his witty wisdom and practical helps. One piece of advice he gave centers on this third character-based truth:

> Learn the skill of reflection, which is the act of pondering life's events with the intent of learning from them. I call this process "rerunning the tapes." . . .
>
> At the end of the day take a few moments to review the happenings of the day—where you went, what you did, what you said. Ponder what worked and what didn't, what you want to repeat and what you want to avoid. . . .
>
> It's not what happens to a person that makes the difference in how his or her life turns out. Rather, it's what he or she does with what happens.[5]

Of course, his comment about "rerunning the tapes" made more sense to people back when we actually had tapes, but it's still a valid point today. To reach our potential in developing our character, we must carve out time for reflection, for review, for insight. We must ask ourselves the questions no one else will ask us: How well did we live up to our values today? How did we spend our time when we were alone? How did we add value to those we encountered? Are we pleased by the actions we took?

Our director of client coaching at Unlocking Potential, Jeffrey Richardson, spends a good portion of his time helping one leader or another untangle a variety of knots. These men and women will say to Jeffrey, "I'm not sure I'm in the right organization" or "I'm not certain I'm in the right role." They'll question whether they're operating at full capacity, or whether they're doing all they can do to support their teams. They'll probe the work/home balance. They'll check in regarding their personal growth. And though I don't relish the fact that these clients are troubled when they call, I do applaud the reflection that is evident in their questions. There is no way they could be in touch with these vexing issues unless they were contemplating deep things about themselves and their place in the world. Thoughtful reflection is on their side, and it will take them far.

Winston Churchill, the prime minister who led Britain to victory in World War II, often stole away during stressful seasons for quiet moments—just himself and his cigar.

My mom often pulled away after her responsibilities for the day were done and worked on a piece of art.

For many years now, my practice has included waking in the early-morning hours—to sit, to pray, to think. I've found that if it doesn't happen then, it doesn't happen at all. Once I'm engaged in the day's work, I tend not to slow down as the day wears on. That may be one reason why the campaign trail was such a challenge for me. On many of those days, I needed to be *on* by 6:00 a.m., which left precious little time to pull away from life to reflect. I joyfully met the demands of that months-long experience, but I sure loved returning to my morning routine.

My point is simply that the people of impact I know carve out time away from life's hustle and grind to simply sit a spell with their thoughts. They understand the value of replaying the tapes, of reviewing, of assessing, of solitude. Another thing they all seem to grasp? The practice of reflection cannot be rushed.

Rushing around like a headless chicken may be a way of life for some people, but it doesn't have to be for you. I know this can be especially difficult these days, when some blinking, buzzing, chiming piece of technology is always close at hand, demanding our immediate attention. Reflection brings its own reward, but it requires putting distractions aside.

I'm not handing you an expectation as much as an *invitation*: Pull back from your usual obligations—for an hour, ten minutes, three breaths. Reflect on the day you've just finished or the one you're about to begin; think about the conversations you've had, the flashes of insight that rushed through your mind. Sit with those thoughts and explore what they mean. Turn them over in your mind like gems. Invest a commute, or a walk, or a bath as a time for simple reflection. Take up journaling. Practice prayer. After you've tried this a few times, see if you don't feel more centered, more gracious, more aligned with your desired self. See if you're beginning to approach interactions with others differently, as one who is more patient, more open, more at ease. See if you don't make key decisions differently, now that you've added a boost of thoughtfulness to your world.

Back when I was hip-deep in corporate life, I remember noticing that the higher I went up the ladder, the more pressure there was to make decisions *for* other people—and consequential decisions, at that. I learned to practice what I call a "pre-decision pause." When I felt myself being pressured for a decision of significance, instead of rushing to judgment and blurting out a yes or no, I would say, very calmly and plainly, "I'm not ready to make a decision." I would request the extension I thought was necessary— another hour, another day, another week—to come to a confident choice, and I would suggest we reconvene at that time.

Sometimes, I have felt great pressure to please people by answering quickly just because someone was waiting to hear. I've learned to take whatever time I need to make a wise and thoughtful decision. During that time, I seek guidance. I reflect. I think. I pray.

You might experiment with a pre-decision pause yourself. The next time you're tempted to react in the moment, close your mouth and take a measured breath. Stop whatever you're doing and fall totally silent. Think. Evaluate. Don't respond.

The scenario could be as mundane as your kid pushing your buttons over a house rule you're trying to enforce. When you get some back talk, you may be tempted to fly off the handle, issue threats, or dole out punishment. Instead, *stop*. Close your mouth. Gather your power and keep it for yourself. Don't give it away in the form of shouting or ranting or going nuts. Blink. Breathe. Pause. Tell that (wonderful, marvelous, gift-from-God) child that you need a little time to reflect on what has been said or done. Tell him or her that you'll be back in touch in a minute/an hour/a day. Seek guidance from other parents whose kids are older or grown— moms and dads who aren't in the thick of child-rearing, who have perspective, who are rested, who smile! Sit with the situation. Think. Keep your wits about you. Stay true to your values. Stand down in the face of impulsivity. Refuse the temptation to do, do, do, respond, respond, respond. You will not regret this measured approach, I promise you. You're bringing sanity back to your life.

Don't always respond immediately to the tweet or the Facebook post, Instagram, or email. Why must you? Pause. Think. Steady yourself. As time passes, you may decide that no answer is the best answer of all. And if you do respond, your answer will have far more impact; it will be thoughtful and deliberate, not rushed and thoughtless.

Remember: Taking a few moments (or longer) to contemplate the right decision is a sign of great leadership and great maturity. It's also a sign that you're still on the path.

4. The more we manifest strength of character, the stronger our character becomes.

Building character is a self-perpetuating process, not unlike the effect of muscle on the human frame. When you strengthen your biceps, for example, your arm gets stronger, which allows you to lift more weight than before. When you strengthen your character muscle, your honor gets stronger, which allows you to prevail in more challenging tests. My suggestion, if you're looking to kick-start this process, is to start light, as you would with weights.

If your employer is counting on you to work an honest eight-hour day, you lift those character-building weights each time you choose to stay off social media while on the clock.

If your child is enduring a stressful season at school,

you lift those character-building weights each time you choose to seek help for him or her without judgment or condemnation.

If you have received a scary or daunting health diagnosis, you lift those character-building weights each time you choose to straighten your spine, push back your shoulders, and face a new day with hope.

As you set your mind, your heart, and your will on choosing integrity, you will become the person of character you long to be.

I'm not one for making baseless promises, and I can confidently guarantee this: As you set your mind, your heart, and your will on choosing integrity, as time goes on you will become the person of character you long to be. Choose to respond with integrity to the challenges you face. Choose to engage with integrity in your relationships. Let good character (which is integrity over the long haul, remember?) have its way.

Let's review the four axioms again:

1. Character is critical when the going gets tough. (And the going always gets tough.)
2. Contrary to popular opinion, the ends never justify the means.
3. Character demands reflection, and reflection can't be rushed.
4. The more we manifest strength of character, the stronger our character becomes.

As you scan this list, I wonder which entry gives you the most pause, and why. Have you been living with a sense of entitlement, believing that life owes you more than it has delivered? Have you been hyperfocused on your short game at the expense of a long-term view? Are your relationships suffering from lack of trust? Do you need to choose integrity more consistently? When was the last time that you truly pulled away to reflect on your heart and your life? Have you been staying the course when it comes to your character, remembering that you're in training, just like at the gym?

I encourage you to linger with the axioms that seem most relevant to you right now. Resolve today to let character be your guide. Resolve today to manifest courage, to pursue peace, to tell the truth. As you pursue integrity, in these and countless other ways, your power will be multiplied. Just you watch. The choices you make today will pay big dividends.

chapter seven

BECOMING A
BETTER *US*

Sharing Your Power

You AND I have probably never met, and yet there is something we share. Whether you are a recent college graduate scanning the employment horizon, résumé ready and fingers crossed that you'll land a job; a twentysomething political activist who dreams of brighter days; a forty-five-year-old freelancer determined to steer clear of corporate life; a retired mentor-type eager to pass wisdom to the generations coming behind you—whoever you are, wherever you've been, and wherever you're headed in coming days, here is what I know about you: Like me, you're endeavoring to thrive in a whole new world, a world driven by technology that did not even exist fifteen years ago.

Though the first commercially available smartphone— the Simon Personal Communicator—debuted in 1992, the result of an IBM developer tinkering around, most students of contemporary culture point to June 29, 2007, as the date when everything changed. That was the day the first iPhone was released. Over the next six months, Apple sold 1.39 million units—but that was only the beginning.[1] According to Statista, Apple sold 41.3 million iPhones worldwide in the third quarter of 2018, after selling almost 217 million units in fiscal 2017.[2] Though at the outset it looked like nothing more than a shiny, harmless device, its effect on our minds and hearts has proved significant. The impact is hardly benign.

For the first time in human history, anyone can access

almost any piece of information, from anywhere in the world. For the first time in human history, digital communication has replaced all things analog, and *mobility* is now a given for us. For the first time in human history, we have more control over our surroundings than ever before—and yet aren't *we* sometimes the ones being controlled?

I'm sure you've had the experience of sitting at a table in a restaurant and glancing over at a couple seated nearby, ostensibly out on a date. It's obvious they invested real time and energy getting ready for the special occasion, and yet there they sit across from each other, engrossed in their individual phones.

Maybe they're texting each other?

That would be better than the alternatives, I suppose. But I'm pretty sure they're not.

Maybe you've been on a "date" like that.

Maybe you've stepped out into traffic while staring at your GPS app.

Maybe you've spent hours "InstaEditing," determined to get just the right look.

Maybe you fall asleep at night with earbuds in, putting off the terror of silence until the last possible moment of your waking day.

New Yorker magazine contributor Joshua Rothman calls modern-age distraction a "universal competency" and says, "We're all experts."[3] He may be closer to the truth than he knows: A recent study cites one in eight Americans as suffering from "problematic Internet use," broadening the definition of addictive behavior to include "cybersex and online porn; video gaming; gambling; eBay and other online auctions or shopping; social media; excessive texting [and] smartphone overuse."[4]

In case you're distancing yourself from such outright *addicts*, I'm curious: Would you pass the screening for IAD—Internet Addiction Disorder? According to Dr. Kimberly Young, Dr. David Greenfield, and others who have researched such things, the signs of a technology addiction include the following:

- You feel preoccupied with the Internet (meaning you think about previous online activity or anticipate the next online session).
- You feel the need to use the Internet for increasing amounts of time to achieve satisfaction.
- You feel restless, moody, depressed, or irritable when attempting to cut down or stop Internet use.
- You stay online longer than originally intended.
- You use technology as a way of escaping problems or relieving feelings of helplessness, guilt, anxiety, or depression.
- You feel the need to respond immediately to your smartphone.
- You constantly check the phone even when it does not ring or vibrate. (Phantom vibration, or thinking the phone vibrates when it hasn't, is a real phenomenon.)
- You ignore what's happening in real time in favor of what's happening in the virtual world. [There's our date-night couple. *Hello?* You're on a *date*.]
- You feel anxious when away from your device or computer.[5]

I don't really understand this last one. Most digital natives never feel this type of anxiety. They're *never* away from their phones.

Don't get me wrong; I enjoy the staggeringly robust features of my smartphone as much as any user out there, and yet I am quick to acknowledge what it cannot do. It cannot make me *smarter*, for example. It cannot improve my ability to focus. It cannot lengthen my attention span. It cannot reduce my sense of entitlement from having information delivered to me on my own terms and at my own convenience. It cannot grow new brain cells for me. It cannot teach me the blessing of patience. It cannot inject sanity into the pace of my life. What's more—and closer to the topic at hand—it does not help me relate better with other people.

As I survey what we human beings have become over the past twelve years, I find it's nothing to brag about. We have become more thoughtless and careless. We have become more intolerant, more bullying, more crass. We have elevated superficiality over substance, lauding people who are famous for being famous over those who contribute depth and beauty to the world. We prize the salacious, the scandalous, the outrageous, the controversial, and the divisive. Worse yet, we seem to have no remorse or regret over these emerging trends.

Despite plentiful evidence to the contrary, some people seem to believe that true fulfillment is found in more "followers" or "likes per minute." We think our lives will be enhanced by knowing what some self-identified celebrity ate for dinner last night, or what color her hair is today. We buy into the idea that Fantasy Football is the stuff of dreams. We try to quantify the health of our relational world by tabulating "virtual friends." And yet don't we all acknowledge that a moment of reckoning is coming—or perhaps is already here? Collectively, we don't want to face it, fearing our worlds will come crashing down. But in our hearts, we're certain that the ways we've been scratching our inner itch have left us even itchier than we were before.

As it relates to our ability to "find our way," relational itchiness plays a key role. As we seek to stay the course toward our fullest potential, while keeping our feet firmly planted on the path, it's one thing to master our inner world—overcoming fear, manifesting courage, carving out time for earnest reflection, sticking to our values when the going gets tough—but it's another thing entirely to master these skills in our outward relationships. Especially when other people don't cooperate. But master these skills we must, if we ever hope to thrive.

Crafting sustainable solutions over the long haul requires committed partnerships with others who are as eager for change as are we. Solving real-world problems demands collaboration—there's no way around it. Nothing of lasting value happens with an individual person acting alone; it takes an *us* to succeed.

I think you'll agree that any problem worth solving is a problem that affects more than just you. An issue in your marriage is one that affects both you and your spouse. An issue with a colleague at work is one that impacts you and that person. An issue with your child's teacher affects the three of you—at least. Even a health issue within your own body touches not just you, but your friends and family as well. Likewise, one person's addiction matters significantly to loved ones and others.

Just as political power concentrated for too long in too few hands is destined to be abused, the same dynamic applies to you and me. When we isolate and insulate, hoarding our power and refusing to share, that power becomes an untended flame in our hands, eventually burning up everything in sight. Certainly, we mustn't give away our power indiscriminately—as we do when we forsake courage and cave in to fear—but when we thoughtfully, willingly, and enthusiastically offer our power for the benefit of the group, that's when real progress can occur.

Every problem is a shared problem; shared power is what will get it solved.

People never disappoint me.

Whenever I make this statement—as I often do—in meetings and in one-on-one conversations, it always seems to catch folks off guard. They think I'm being flippant, foolish, or both. In fact, the opposite is true.

Whenever I say that people never disappoint me, I'm being completely honest. And here's what I mean: I'm convinced, from decades of enlightening experiences, that absolutely any problem can be solved with the right people around the table. When the right mix of experience, perspective, expertise, and attention to detail comes together, there's nothing that team cannot accomplish.

I have been in countless meetings that came to a stalemate over a particular issue. But rather than becoming frustrated, or feeling helpless, hopeless, or enraged, I've learned to say to myself, "We're missing someone we need."

We needed one more person's perspective.

We needed one more person's passion.

We needed one more person's logic.

We needed one more person's levity.

We needed one more person's optimism.

We needed one more person's pragmatism.

We needed one more person's *something*—a something we did not have.

Diversity of opinion is the dynamite that blows up the logjams that are keeping groups stuck. But how do we manage all that diversity? Two words: *humility* and *empathy*. When those two qualities are evident, true collaboration becomes possible.

Now that selfies rule the world, we don't venerate the character qualities of humility and empathy much anymore. Many psychotherapists and cultural researchers believe that selfies have quite a detrimental effect on social-media consumers—tweens, teens, and twentysomethings in particular.

Whenever I travel, whether around the country or around the world, I'm amazed by how many people seem to be engaged in consistently focusing on themselves. Instead of seeing and experiencing the majesty of the Grand Canyon, the beauty of a seashore, or the throbbing excitement of Times Square, they're posing for selfies. How much *more* are they missing?

Legendary basketball coach Phil Jackson defines the essence of *esprit de corps* as "the ability to incorporate other beings in your plans, in your system."[6] That's collaboration. Renowned clinical psychologist Dr. Henry Cloud says that our willingness to become an "open system"—that is, to "open yourself to outside feedback, input, coaching, information, and energy"—is critical to our ability to increase in integrity, to live lives in which our values and actions align.[7] Dr. Cloud defines such openness as the propensity to join forces with those outside ourselves, with people who lovingly push us to develop and grow. Might I humbly suggest a viable starting point for this commendable way of life?

PUT DOWN YOUR PHONE!

To experience effective collaboration, we must commit ourselves to practice humility and empathy. To practice humility and empathy, we must step outside the bounds of ourselves first, and then outside of our own little tribes. It's human nature to want to be with our own people, our kind, our squad. It's easier, often more fun, and always more comfortable to spend our time with people like us. And yet, if we want to make a difference, we must approach and engage with people who think, look, and act differently. We must be willing to say to the world at large, "I recognize that I don't have all the answers." (That's humility.) "And I acknowledge that you can help me fill in those gaps." (That's empathy.) Humility is the understanding that *we can't go it alone*. Empathy is the ability to identify with the challenges that have brought other people to where they are. Combined, these two traits invite us into authentic relationships with others, allowing collaborative energy to begin to flow. Humility keeps us open to new information, new insights, new wisdom. Empathy encourages us to unite.

Before we move on, allow me to share with you three phrases I've learned that will help you as you seek to become more collaborative:

- *I long to learn.*
- *I crave connection.*
- *I refuse to go it alone.*

Try repeating these phrases to yourself to help you focus on collaboration with others.

What is humility, and why does it matter?

Organizational psychologist Adam Grant once posed an interesting question to former NBA player Shane Battier, who won two NBA titles with the Miami Heat during a fourteen-year career playing for three different teams. Grant asked, "How do you make your team better when you're not the biggest star?"[8]

How do you make your team better when you're not the biggest star?

By way of context, the Heat had attempted to build a championship-caliber team in 2010 by recruiting superstar free agents LeBron James and Chris Bosh to join with resident Heat superstar Dwyane Wade. The trio became known as "the Big Three," and they had high aspirations. Speaking at a preseason press conference that year, LeBron James famously promised multiple championships: "Not two, not three, not four, not five, not six, not seven."[9] But that plan was foiled from the start. The threesome, falling prey to the age-old problems that arise whenever too many cooks are in the kitchen, not only failed to win a ring that first year, they also failed to win some regular-season games they should have won.

Something needed to change.

Now, if you were to ask many organizational managers what they would recommend in such a situation, a common theme you'd hear would be to *aim high*, *get the best talent available*, and *go for broke*. But that's not what the Heat chose to do. Instead, they went after Shane Battier, who was then playing for the Houston Rockets and was hardly considered a superstar.

Bestselling author Michael Lewis once described Battier's game as "a weird combination of obvious weaknesses and nearly invisible strengths."[10] He didn't grab a lot of rebounds or take a lot of shots, but whenever he was on the court, his teammates got better. On defense, he always seemed to draw the other team's best player; and though he didn't necessarily shut them down, he managed to significantly reduce their shooting percentage.[11]

This wasn't merely a perception regarding Shane Battier. Statistically, these things were all true. His teammates played better when Shane was on the court than when Shane was seated on the bench.

How was this possible? In Shane's own words: "You do that by doing all the things that no one else wants to do. For me, that was the exciting plays like diving for loose balls, taking charges, running back on defense, being the most enthusiastic, being the most communicative, being a great teammate."[12] In other words, he fueled his humility instead of his pride. He didn't embrace false modesty. He didn't pretend to be less important than he was. He simply played for a cause greater than inflating his own ego. He played for the good of the team.

What a freeing approach to life!

To nobody's surprise, the Miami Heat won the NBA Championship the next two seasons—and all the glory went to the Big Three. But I'm telling you, those championships were fueled by the team-first guy who made everyone around him better.

When a team is not firing on all cylinders, the first gauge to check is the one that measures humility. The most impactful people I've known have all embraced the truth of the Latin phrase *sic transit gloria mundi*: "Thus passes the glory of the world." They've understood that earthly adoration is fleeting and not worth staking our lives on.

To be humble is to be teachable. It is to play the role that others don't want to play. It is to find comfort in admitting that we don't always know. It is to seek out opportunities to learn. From what I've observed in life, either we seek out humility, or humility will find us. Back at AT&T, when I was first promoted to officer, I had high hopes for overseeing manufacturing, operations, or some other "real" line of work. Instead, I was assigned to the strategy division.

Strategy! What kind of fluff gig is that! Why were they sidelining me?

In fairness to my higher-ups there, strategy is a very important part of any successful corporation, and it's quite difficult to do well. It's just that organizations as a whole rarely value strategy, which meant I faced an uphill climb. In some respects, I'd been promoted to "professional nag." As some would say, it was a job for a woman. Manufacturing, not so much.

The way I saw it, I had a choice to make. I could stew and sulk and slide right into a self-fulfilling prophecy of irrelevance and disregard. Or I could work to make the strategy division valuable by the way I lived and led. I chose the latter and plowed ahead.

Though I never succeeded in winning over certain portions of the company that insisted on doing their own thing, that "strategy gig" turned into a wild blessing for me. There, I learned so much about how people operate. The strategy division spanned every part of the organization, and my role demanded that I help shape the plans for all those groups. Out of sheer necessity, then, I learned to forge and deepen relationships; I learned to ask questions to understand other people's points of view; and I learned to prize other people's success. I look back on that experience and think, *Where else would I have gained all that learning?* What a gift. Truly, a gift. And I'm amazed to think that if I had "stayed on plan," I would have missed out on a very valuable piece of the path for me.

I have a friend who lives by many brilliant axioms. "Go where you can learn" is one that I have also embraced. Move toward the person who has a different life experience. Move toward those topics you know nothing about. Move toward the stimulating conversations at the dinner party, even if you feel you have nothing to add. Move toward the challenging book. Move toward the networking conference. Move toward the situations and stories that stir your mind and your soul. Choose to go where you can learn.

Either we can choose humility, or humility will one day choose us. Far better to *intentionally* assume the posture of a learner, to ask questions, to admit what you do not know. You know the old proverb: "Pride goeth . . . before a fall."[13]

Earlier, I mentioned the commencement speech I gave at North Carolina A&T shortly after I left HP. What I didn't mention was that, a few days after that speech, I flew to New England to address the student body of an Ivy League school. In North Carolina, the students had been rapt as I delivered my remarks, thoroughly engaged, eager to listen, and eager to learn. Many were quite literally perched on the edge of their seats, as if they were saying, "Give us every ounce of wisdom you can!" They were prepared. They were energized. They were grateful. They were "open systems," one and all.

Quite a contrast to the Ivy League audience. When I stepped to the podium, I could see their collective expression of self-satisfaction. They seemed ill-prepared to listen. Apathetic. Bored to tears. Annoyed. In the words of country-music singer Tim McGraw, their countenance said loud and clear, "Can't tell me nothin'. . . ."

We missed out on a powerful shared experience that day because only one of us came prepared to engage. Without humility, you can't learn from others—and you certainly can't collaborate to solve problems.

What is empathy, and why does it matter?

For all its importance, humility is only half of the collaboration equation. The other half, of course, is empathy—the ability to lend understanding to someone who is different from you.

If you have ever been late to a meeting because you logged the incorrect start time in your calendar, and a member of the meeting looked at you, smiled, and said, "No worries, we've all done it," then you have been the recipient of empathy. If you've ever articulated your position on a delicate topic, and the person to whom you were speaking said, "I understand what you are saying," or if you've confessed an embarrassing habit or addiction to a friend and heard that friend say, "I've been there too," then you have seen empathy in action. If you've ever stood up for someone or something and heard, "I appreciate your perspective" in response; or if you've ever expressed dissatisfaction with a spouse or a friend and heard, "I'm so sorry to hear that" in reply, then you have seen empathy at work.

"Empathy is a choice," says research professor Brené Brown, "and it's a vulnerable choice. Because in order to connect with you, I have to connect with something in myself that knows that feeling."[14] Such a worthwhile aspiration! Such a challenge to execute.

Truly, the coping distance between our typical hair-on-fire pace and the thoughtful, intentional, generous expression Dr. Brown suggests can feel most days like traversing the Grand Canyon. On foot. Without shoes. In the rain. Is there any hope for us?

I spoke at a university gathering in 2018, and partway through my opener, which I thought was lighthearted and expectant and fun, out of the corner of my eye I caught a glimpse of three young women in the fourth or fifth row standing to their feet. They reached underneath their seats for the poster boards they'd brought. "Eat the rich," one of the signs said. "Your white feminism sucks," read another. "Human need, not corporate greed," read the third.

Ah, so it's going to be one of those nights.

I greeted the women and read their signs aloud, so I was clear on what they'd come to say. Then I asked if they would be willing to stay through my talk until the floor was open for Q&A. I genuinely welcomed the spirited discourse I imagined we'd have. But unfortunately, we didn't get a chance to have that conversation. The women refused to sit down so I could carry on with my talk, and eventually they were asked to leave.

In my view, their behavior was a tangible display of the temptation we all face these days, which is to holler out our five-word protest while refusing to listen to the other side. What we have in our society today is a breakdown of empathy—of gigantic proportions. We'll never make progress this way.

If we hope to come together instead of driving each other apart, we must commit with equal passion to the practices of humility and empathy. Let's look at how to do that.

From time to time, when I talk with clients of our Leadership Lab about the qualities of humility and empathy, many of the men in the room subtly groan. In a flash, I've lost half the group. But before they can reach for their smartphones and tune me out, I say, "Ah, so you think these things are feminine qualities. They're not. They're human qualities, but only the strongest among us can manifest them. It takes far more strength to be teachable and others-focused than to be bombastic and soaked in ourselves."

Usually it takes a moment for the guys to come around, but once they rejoin the group emotionally, we start to make real progress, because they, too, want to experience a greater sense of connectivity—in both their professional and personal lives. What I find in those wide-ranging audiences is that the reason they're not excelling in collaborative relationships is because they've never understood why humility and empathy are important, or they haven't been taught how to develop and use them.

How to Display Humility and Empathy: A Guide

Earlier I mentioned my talented associate Casey, who is in her twenties. Only recently has she begun to establish genuine humility in her communication style. This isn't a criticism of her. For years, fearing that older businesspeople would look down on her because of her age and comparative lack of experience, Casey worked to prove herself in meetings by speaking up before she really had something to say, by putting pressure on herself to "look smart," and by second-guessing every response she received. It was a stressful dynamic, to say the least.

She and I had countless conversations about the early days of my own career, when I knew zilch about business and even less about social intelligence. My solution was simply to ask questions, to try to learn something new, and to put myself in someone else's shoes. Eventually, Casey decided to give this approach a try. Instead of feeling pressure to speak up about every topic in every meeting, she began asking questions to seek clarity. Instead of striving to be noticed, she worked to really see the others in the room. Instead of hyperanalyzing every word and nonverbal cue, she stayed present with the conversation at hand.

"I feel like I've reclaimed so much of my power," she tells me today, "which makes my contribution strong and sure."

If you want to know whether the value of collaboration is functioning in your life, try asking yourself the following questions during a time of reflection and introspection. Where might you need to improve?

1. In conversations with others, do I come off as a know-it-all?
2. Am I capable of doing a good deed and not telling a soul about it?
3. Am I okay hanging around people who are wiser and/or more accomplished than I am?
4. Am I prone to "negotiate truth" so that I come out looking good?
5. Do I insist on being "special," or am I willing to fight for the collective good?
6. Do I truly value people, or do I tend to use them toward my own ends?
7. Do I spend more time and energy bragging on myself or bragging on others?
8. Am I more likely to blame someone else for the predicaments I find myself in or to take responsibility for them myself?

9. Am I generally a good listener, or do I frequently feel the tension of wanting to get my words in?
10. Would those who know me best describe me more as climbing some sort of ladder, or as going down the ladder to help others find their way up?

Now, to empathy. In our selfie-saturated world, if you were to implement only one action item from this chapter, here's the one I suggest you put at the top of your list: Stash your smartphone and start engaging more intentionally with the people around you. You will not build empathy by staring at a five-and-a-half-inch screen. Empathy is all about *connecting* with people in the real world.

To gauge my level of empathy, I find it useful to scrutinize my motivations from time to time. "Based on the thoughts I'm thinking, the words I'm speaking, and the questions I'm asking," I'll ask myself, "am I more committed these days to judging others or to understanding them?"

I was in a management-training class once that focused on the nuances of international business, and my instructor made an interesting point about how punctuality is prioritized in various cultures. My experience in North American business had taught me to be on time to every meeting, lest I send an unintended signal of disrespect. My husband is especially fanatical about this practice, which means that I'm generally not only on time but early. But in Latin America, where we were starting to do quite a bit of business, the instructor explained that to show up on time for a business meeting was exceedingly rude. If a meeting was scheduled for 10:00 a.m., for example, you should show up at 10:30 or even 11:00.

This information was revelatory for me because it dealt with far more than time management. Hidden in the recesses of my heart, I had formed an assumption that our colleagues in Latin America were disrespectful, negligent, and even unfit for leadership, as evidenced by their seeming inability to show up for meetings or log into conference calls at the stated start time. Punctuality is the American way, right? Not for all of America, it turns out.

To genuinely empathize with another person or group, we must see things the way they see them. Which brings me to three useful principles that will help you grow in understanding and empathy.

A bedrock principle of our nation's founding was the "self-evident truth" that people matter above all else. Though we haven't always practiced it perfectly down through the years, this belief is central to our society nonetheless. That's why the Constitution was written to value people over institutions. People over governments. People over hierarchies. People over organizational structures. People over all else.

People over all else. As it turns out, this principle is also at the heart of empathy. So how do we do a better job of practicing this priority? Three ideas:

1. *Stop avoiding the people you've been avoiding.* Are there are people, or people groups, you tend to avoid? Maybe the neighbor whose dog always runs through your garden? Maybe the person from a different part of the world, whose accent you can't

quite understand? Perhaps the woman at work who is perpetually trying to sell you something—her ideas, her side business, her approach to life? Or is it the family member you refuse to sit next to at Thanksgiving dinner? Cigarette smokers? People on drugs? People with tattoos? Homeschool families? Democrats? Republicans? If you'd like a surefire way to hone your empathy skills, stop avoiding these people and draw near. Make an effort to understand where they're coming from.

2. *See before you speak.* As you approach conversation with the people you've been avoiding, remember the three phrases I suggested earlier:

- *I long to learn.*
- *I crave connection.*
- *I refuse to go it alone.*

  Before you say a single word, *see* the other person. Stop and really observe him or her. It's possible to *look* without seeing and to *listen* without hearing—so *focus* and *tune in.* When I meet someone for the first time, or when I start a conversation with someone I already know, I try to pause before speaking to look at the person's eyes, even for just a beat. That flash of intentional connection has changed the course of many conversations. So before you notice a person's outer adornment—the hair, the glasses, the trappings, the clothes—notice his or her eyes. If the eyes are a window to the soul, they're a good place to

start in making an empathetic connection with
other people.

3. *Clarify, don't criticize.* Once you do open your mouth
to speak, start with a *question*, not a statement.
Collaborative people are forever asking questions—
questions that probe the other person's experience,
questions that scan the relational horizon for
common ground, questions that build up instead
of tearing down. The key is to ask questions that
clarify rather than criticize. Suppose you're enjoying a
long weekend with extended family, and that person
you never get along with is sitting outside reading a
book. A question that clarifies might sound like this:
"I noticed the author you're reading; how are you
enjoying his book?" A question that criticizes might
sound like this: "Why would anyone read anything
by such a flaming liberal?" or "Why are you out
here avoiding everyone?" Now, I'm exaggerating for
effect, but please don't miss the point. We often tend
to ask questions that critique. Empathy is built on
questions that seek to understand.

Allow me to expand on that final point. The questions
we ask have tremendous power. They can be wildly effective
in bringing together people who might otherwise choose to
stay apart. Sometimes the right question comes down to the
words we use. Sometimes the right question comes down to
a simple matter of tone. Think of the difference between asking someone with whom you disagree, "Why do you think

that?" versus "Tell me why you think that," spoken in a tone of genuine curiosity.

A Christian woman named Gayle who lives in Chicago felt self-conscious and unprepared about asking the "right" questions when she encountered Muslims who lived in her neighborhood. Finally, she grew tired of always putting her foot in her mouth and asked her next-door neighbor, who was also a Muslim, for some guidance.

"I want to love all people well, but I'm struggling to find common ground," she admitted.

"I'm happy to help," her neighbor said.

The pair began meeting for coffee once a month, where Gayle could ask clarifying questions in a safe space.

Is it okay to ask a Muslim woman about her hijab? Is it okay to speak to a Muslim woman when she's in the company of her husband? Is it okay to approach her children and engage with them? Are there foods that practicing Muslims cannot eat or places they cannot go?

The neighbor patiently explained her culture and her religion to Gayle and gave her tips about what to say when she encountered Muslims in her daily life.

Eventually the tables turned, and the neighbor began asking questions of Gayle.

Why are there so many Christian denominations? What sets them apart from one another? What are the rules surrounding the tithe? Why do some Christians prioritize disciplines such as fasting and prayer, while others do not?

The two women have been meeting for more than four years now, and each time they come together, they carve out a deeper capacity for empathy. It is a worthy endeavor to get over our "fear of the other," whether that otherness centers on politics, religion, ethnicity, lifestyle, or any of a hundred other categories. It's worth it to learn how to ask thoughtful, substantial questions—questions that draw a person out, questions that lift a person up, questions that encourage instead of condemn. Not only will this skill help you to get conversations off the ground, but it will also help you remain civil as the dialogue unfolds.

One of my biggest beefs with the invasion of social media into our lives is the prevalence of vitriol there. If you need a slice of humble pie, just log into Twitter or read the comments after just about any online posting. People say the craziest, meanest things, because there is no real accountability. We can do better than that. We can *be* better. I'm confident of that. Here's a simple starting point for taking the venom out of any interaction: Offer people *feedback*, not criticism.

There is a vast difference between feedback and criticism. Someone who criticizes intends to tear down. We criticize someone's motives, intentions, intelligence, or appearance. We imply that the person we are criticizing isn't as smart, kind, pretty, or "woke" as we are.

Someone who gives feedback intends to lift up. We all need feedback sometimes—when we've made a mistake, when we could be better. But feedback comes from people who care about you and want you to be better. Feedback doesn't impugn your motives or question your character or intellect.

Criticism, on the other hand, feels like a grenade has landed in your lap. It demands an urgent reaction, and you're aware that things might blow up. Nobody likes to be criticized. Even the most critical trolls on social media don't like to be criticized. Tossing an online verbal grenade can feel pretty satisfying in the moment; but do you see how counterproductive it is? It takes no courage whatsoever to toss an anonymous grenade; in fact, cowardice is always the grenade launcher. You can't practice strength of character while you're laying into people left and right. And collaboration is most definitely not happening when we're blowing each other to shreds.

Oprah Winfrey and I have had some wonderful conversations together. Years ago, it was Oprah who taught me not to read the negative things that were written about me, the unwelcome and harsh critiques. That doesn't mean I can fully protect myself, given how many rude things have been said right to my face, but I have found that not searching online for my name, for instance, helps me to have a more pleasant day. What's more, whenever I encounter in-person awfulness, I can choose not to engage. I can choose to remain civil instead of caving in to retaliation. I can choose to offer feedback instead of criticism. I can choose to be a whole lot easier to be around.

These are the kinds of choices you can make too.

You can engage others with generosity of spirit and graciousness of heart—even those who know where your buttons are and seem to delight in pushing them.

You can say to your spouse, "You're such a responsible person that I'm sure it would feel good for us to be on the same page financially," instead of "I can't believe you spent hundreds of dollars on _____ this month, when we're barely making ends meet!"

You can say to your colleague, "That probably felt awful to get called out in the meeting like that" instead of "You knew that was coming, right?"

You can say to your teenager, "I bet you have a lot of conflicting thoughts and plans swimming through your mind," instead of "You can never make a decision. You're never going to make anything of yourself."

Learning to ask open-ended, empathetic questions teaches us to speak open-ended, empathetic statements, as well. Empathy allows us to make the subtle shift between opening someone up and utterly shutting the person down.

Going All In

During a recent Leadership Lab, I was reminded of how tempting it is to try to fake our way through the cultivation of humility and empathy—collaboration's powerful and necessary twin attributes. The participants had just finished working in breakout groups and were now reporting their results to the full group. When it was one group's turn to address the room, a man I'll call Mark stood up to speak. But instead of delivering a report on the work his team had produced, he chose to simply confess what was on his heart. It was a powerful moment.

"You know," he began, "a lot of the issues raised today have to do with how we brand our company, which, as you all know, is the part of the business I oversee. All day, I have been feigning openness to input on how to do branding better, saying, 'Yeah, yeah! Great idea! Thanks a lot,' whenever people offered a suggestion or thought. I've been telling people all day, 'Sure! Come see me with your ideas. Let's get this branding thing solved!' But the truth is, I don't really want their input. I don't plan to really consider their suggestions. In my heart, my plan is to get through this session, check whatever boxes need to be checked, and then go back to work on Monday and do whatever I want."

The room was uncomfortably silent. This guy was speaking some truth.

"But in this last hour or so," Mark continued, "something shifted for me. In this last small-group session, I caught a glimpse of what is possible if I stop faking and actually engage. I'm not above collaboration. In fact, I *need* you guys. I can see now that the only person I've been fooling these past two days is myself. Now, to our group's presentation . . ."

Spontaneous applause broke out across the room, and some people rose to their feet. I felt as if I were at an AA meeting when someone finally admits they're an alcoholic. I must say, my eyes welled up a bit over Mark's impassioned speech. Based on the progress he'd made that day, great things were in store for him.

My point in telling this story is to remind you that for collaboration to work—and no problem worth solving can be solved by one person acting alone, right?—we must have equal parts humility and empathy. We must make progress on both goals.

Collaboration without humility, as Mark had attempted, is fraudulence. It makes you a fake, and nothing more.

On the flip side, collaboration without empathy is

For collaboration to work, we must have equal parts humility and empathy.

forcefulness—"We know exactly what you need!"—and we're simply trying to steamroll our way through.

Think of all the well-intentioned organizations that send people to developing countries to "help" the people there who are in need. In far too many cases, these organizations let their bleeding hearts lead the way, while failing to collect actual data to support their plans. They never think to sit with the people in need and ask open-ended, empathetic questions about their situations. They don't think to inquire about what resources and services would make a meaningful difference in the people's lives. They fail to challenge their own assumptions about the best approach to take. Consequently, they quite prematurely leap into action—assembling their teams, booking their flights, and loading up crates with paintbrushes and buckets of paint. They then proceed to paint the village's sole building, which has been painted sixteen times before by other well-intentioned but shortsighted groups.

The people in need try to be gracious as they wave goodbye to the work crew, even as they can't help but think, *Gee, learning how to market and sell these vegetables we've been growing sure would have been better than having the school building painted again . . .*

Collaboration without humility is fraudulence. Collaboration without empathy is forcefulness. But collaboration with both traits in play? It's the solution we've been searching for. It's the avenue to reaching our fullest potential. It is the way we help others uncover and unleash their own potential. It is how real problems find real solutions. It is how we beautifully and effectively share our power. When we bring our full power to bear on a challenging situation and allow that power to merge with the full power of others around us—mutually agreeing to govern that shared power with humility and empathy in equal parts—the problems that used to bind us must loosen their grip.

You remember the story of my first client meeting, at the strip club in Washington, DC—the fear I had to overcome; the embarrassment I faced upon entering the club; my horror at watching my colleague, Carl, call women over to do table dances for our client; my utter relief when those women demurred. Well, hours after I returned to the office that day, Carl came sauntering in. No doubt emboldened by the drinks he'd enjoyed over lunch, he walked by my desk, slipped a black garter he'd obtained from one of the dancers onto my coffee mug, and walked on without saying a word.

Once Carl was out of earshot, the man who shared office space with me looked up from his work and said, "That guy's got no class."

I met my colleague's eyes but said nothing. Carl's gesture had said it all. But I did take note of the fact that Carl wasn't as bulletproof as I'd believed. Here was one of his peers subtly distancing himself from Carl; did others in the office feel the same way?

Carl never once brought up the strip-club lunch, but as I mentioned, he started treating me with respect. I suppose that in the same way a fraternity pledge must survive hazing to get into the frat's good graces, I had to live through The Board Room for Carl to know I was there to stay.

About nine months into my tenure in that role at AT&T, Carl approached me and said, "You know, Carly, this isn't such a bad arrangement we've got going here . . ."

The "arrangement" he was referring to was the pattern he and I had established for working clients together. Carl would reel in the new business, and I made sure their telecom needs were fulfilled. Carl's sweet spot was relationships. He had all the right connections and was really good at schmoozing decision makers. Where he lacked expertise was in following through on the clients' actual needs. They had real problems needing to be solved, problems that couldn't be addressed by good ol' boy drinking sprees and table dances—problems that I became equipped and eager to help solve.

We became a great team because, in the end, we were both humble enough to realize we needed each other.

Sometimes, people are amazed that I could work successfully with Carl after the strip-club incident. After all, he was trying to humiliate me and diminish me. Here's the truth: My ignorance of my job and my customers gave me humility. I actually couldn't do my job without Carl. I needed him to introduce me to clients, show me the ropes, and navigate the labyrinth of a giant corporation that I didn't yet know or understand.

Though I was desperately afraid of looking like a fool at that strip club—or worse, failing at my first corporate job—through empathy I came to understand that Carl was afraid too. He was afraid of being unceremoniously dumped after a thirty-year career for a younger, shinier model with an MBA. He was afraid of having the things he was most proud of—his relationships with his customers—tossed aside, and his real and significant accomplishments disregarded.

We became a great team because, in the end, we were both humble enough to realize we needed each other—precisely because we were so different. And we both came to empathize with each other's fears and aspirations. Despite the rockiest of starts, we learned to genuinely care for and respect one another.

When Carl retired, he took me aside and asked me to go to work with him in a new business he was setting up. Though I declined, I was deeply grateful when he looked me in the eye and said, "There is no one I would rather have by my side in the foxhole."

Young women ask me all the time for the "one piece of advice" I'd give them as they enter the workforce. Without exception, I say, "Never hide your light under a bushel basket, and never get a chip on your shoulder." In our context here, we might say it like this: Be proud of the power you wield in this world, and watch for ways to share it with others for the greater good—in your own time, in your own way, and on your own terms. And don't assume the worst about others. There are some truly bad people out there, but most are good people who happen to be afraid of something.

If we want to excel at collaboration, we must become *openers*, through and through. And yet I must warn you: This practice is not for the faint of heart. Collaboration is difficult because relationships are difficult. People are complex. They can be messy. They can say things they don't really mean. But when we set them up for success, there's no reason why they should ever let us down.

Problems are the pavement under our feet as we move toward realizing and activating our fullest potential. When we commit to seeing other people—even those who seem annoying, disrespectful, or downright offensive—not as enemies to be avoided but as prospective partners on that path, we'll begin to realize that collaboration is the best way to release abundant resources for solving the problems we face.

chapter eight

THINK OF THE POSSIBILITIES!

Harnessing Your Power

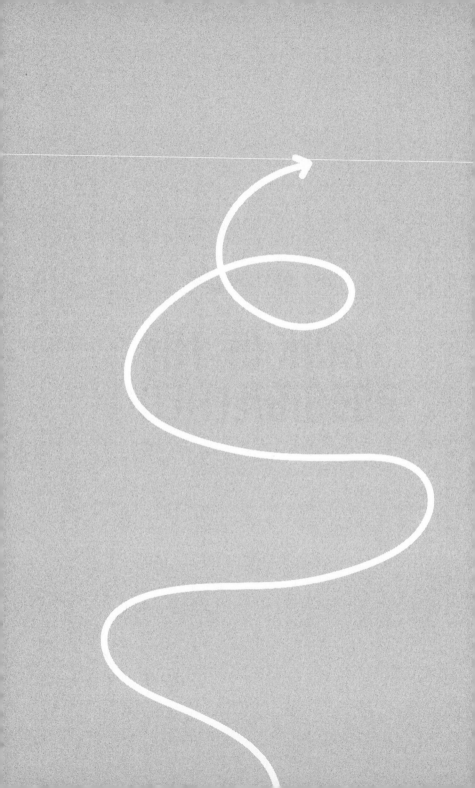

Can I give you one more character quality for building collaboration—one that has saved many a group from certain peril and vast quantities of unnecessary pain? This fourth and final practice, that of *seeing possibilities*, is the ability to envision a better reality than the one you're presently in.

The word *possibilities* conjures all sorts of good things, doesn't it? To think of possibilities is to think of what is available, what is likely, what is imaginable, what is to come. Possibilities encompass the hoped for, the longed for, the optimistic. So let's begin with *optimism*.

Optimism is predisposition to hold on to hope in the face of life's instability; to keep saying yes in a no-plagued world.

General Colin Powell, former chairman of the Joint Chiefs of Staff, astutely describes the quality of optimism as a "force multiplier."[1] That is, a leader's enthusiasm, hopefulness, and confidence will multiply as it radiates outward through an organization.

> *Optimism is a predisposition to hold on to hope in the face of life's instability.*

The opposite is also true: A leader's passivity, despair, and insecurity will multiply as it radiates through an organization. Most likely, at some point in your life, you've been affected by both. Whether it's from a manager, an in-law, a parent, a friend, or a retail clerk, you know what it's like to be influenced by someone's presence and perspective—spanning the full spectrum from anticipation and eagerness to misery, anguish, and gloom. These attitudes and perspectives will either be a breath of fresh air and a shot in the arm, or they'll get on us like secondhand smoke or a piece of gum on the bottom of your shoe.

That's why optimism is so important. If we want to harness the power we've been given; if we want to be a blessing to those with whom we collaborate, we simply must make friends with optimism—the ability to see, and believe, that good things are ahead.

How optimistic are you? Let's look at a few scenarios that will help you gauge your current state of mind.

SCENARIO 1: You decide to dramatically change your eating patterns—to get healthier, to lose weight, to feel more energetic, whatever your motivation may be. You mark off a thirty-day period and are amazed by how well you're sticking to the plan the first three days. On day four, while you're out running errands, minding your own business, you discover that the local bakery is having an anniversary celebration: free doughnut holes! The scent of cinnamon and sugar wafts through the air and assaults your consciousness. Suddenly, you can't resist. You enjoy not one or two, but four doughnut holes. Afterward, do you

(a) feel like a total failure, view this setback as a character flaw, and throw in the towel on your diet because who can succeed in the face of fresh doughnut holes?

(b) view the lapse in self-control as an unfortunate but temporary issue, shrug your shoulders, and resolve to steer clear of the bakery for the rest of the day?

SCENARIO 2: You're in sales for a large manufacturing firm. Your manager stops by your office to congratulate you on the fantastic quarter you've had. "Number one for the entire team!" she gushes, just before telling you what your sizable commission check will likely be. Do you

(a) groan as soon as your manager is out of earshot, thinking, *How am I ever going to meet this new standard I've now set?*

(b) sit back in your chair, exhale a sigh of contentment, and feel grateful that your hard work paid off?

SCENARIO 3: You bump into a friend you haven't seen in quite some time. She asks, "So how are you doing? What's new in your world?" Reflexively, you find yourself answering with

(a) the tough situations you've been dealing with, the struggles, the disappointments, the pain?

(b) the plans you have for this weekend, the trip you're taking next month, the big breakthrough you're anticipating later this year?

If you found yourself gravitating toward the first answer in any of the above scenarios, you may have a bit of work to do to develop an optimistic view of yourself and your life. Still, I hope you'll take heart. There is hope for even a career pessimist to come around. Stick with me, and see if your optimism doesn't go up a few clicks on the dial by the time this chapter concludes.

I have always emphasized the importance of optimism. If a person cannot (or will not) choose to believe that better days will surely dawn, he or she simply cannot move ahead. Optimism is the fuel that allows problem solvers to see things through to the end; however, optimism on its own cannot get us very far. There is a second ingredient necessary for seeing possibilities—namely, a healthy dose of clear-eyed realism. Realism sees what is true of things today. Optimism sees what could be better. We need both.

Years ago, while working in the strategy division at AT&T, I employed a simple—but not easy—tool to help people get the realism/optimism balance right. I called it "current state/ future state," and I have used it countless times since. Want to give it a try?

The practice of seeing possibilities begins with a problem rearing its head. Admittedly, this is the easiest part of the drill. We face problems on every side just getting out of bed in the morning. But the problems we're hoping to prioritize are those that affect more than just us, more than just our isolated corner of the world. So, that lock of gray hair that appeared from nowhere? The blinking Check Engine light on your car? The resentment you've been feeling lately about having to cook dinner every night? Though these may, in fact, be problems for you, they're not exactly the kind I mean.

Instead, let's focus our attention on the broader issues that are hindering meaningful progress for you and those in your sphere. What relational fractures are gobbling precious energy and time? What habits aren't serving your group well? Which systems are derailing your family's ability to have

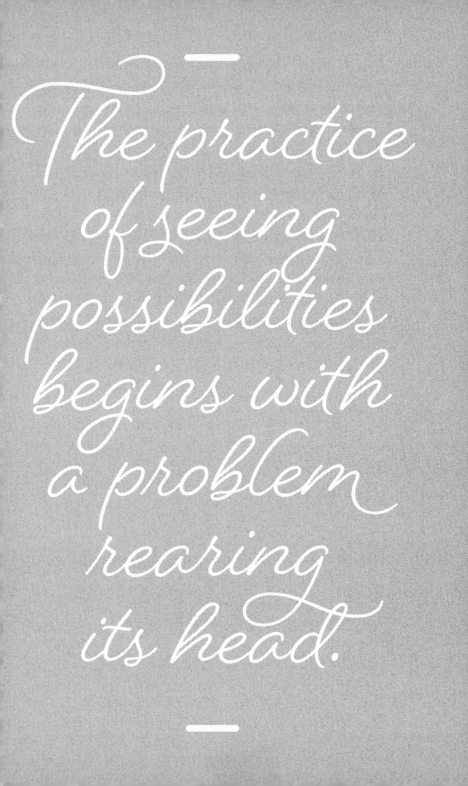

The practice of seeing possibilities begins with a problem rearing its head.

quality time? How is a lack of passion hamstringing your volunteer team? How often is your department scrambling to complete projects? Why do you and your spouse seem unable to abide by the budget you've set? What is keeping your teenager and his or her friends stuck in a spiral of apathy? How might you inspire your girls'-night-out friends to pursue a cause beyond yourselves?

You may not know the exact problems you're supposed to solve during this season, but I'm willing to bet you're aware of certain stress points. You know when communication is strained. You know when deadlines aren't being met. You know where breakdowns are occurring. You know when things aren't working right. For part one of this assessment, all I'm asking you to do is write down your current state. When you *stop*, *look*, and *listen*, what problems bubble up? Don't work to solve these problems just yet; simply get them logged.

- My husband and I are ships passing in the night, and we and the kids are suffering as a result.
- Half the people in my department couldn't care less if we sink or swim.
- Our residential community isn't very communal at all. We all live such siloed lives.
- My friends and I are blessed with plentiful resources, yet we never invest them in anyone else.

Grab a piece of paper, and jot down the key problems plaguing you today. As you list your problems, remember to choose ones that you can actually affect. For example, don't write down "world hunger." Instead, remember Austin Perine, the little boy whose problem was the homeless people he saw in his neighborhood who needed something to eat.

What issues are keeping you up at night? What dilemmas are causing you worry or grief? In case you haven't put the pieces together yet, I'm asking you to define your *current state*—reality as it stands today.

Now comes the fun part: applying *optimism* to start seeing possibilities.

Take one of the problems on your current-state list: What would your dream scenario be? If you could alter reality to create a totally different state of affairs, what would that ideal include?

Let me start with a silly, trivial example to get things rolling. A few months ago, my colleague Casey got a new dog. I should mention that I love dogs and that I'm the proud owner of two adorable dogs myself. I should further mention that Casey's new dog, a Jack Russell mix named Jake, was adopted from a shelter that took him in after he had been mistreated or abused. Naturally, we all wanted to extend grace to sweet little Jake. We wanted him to feel safe and accepted and loved.

Early on, Casey decided to bring Jake to work with her because she was worried he'd freak out if left on his own. His past negative experiences mixed with long hours without attention would probably result in an unfortunate situation, and no one wanted that. So, into the office came Jake each day, which meant he was around . . . a lot.

All was well with Jake in our midst, except for one little

thing. He had trouble discerning the proper location for relieving himself—meaning he didn't know it should be exclusively outdoors. Everyone in the office was soon aware of the problem; but until we could envision the future state we desired, there was only grunting and grumbling and rage. We knew Jake was trainable. We knew that better (drier) days would surely dawn. We just had to believe and keep moving toward our goal.

The *future state* my colleagues and I envisioned centered on Jake's taking care of business outdoors—*predictably* I believe was the word we used. As soon as we declared our goal, we began to establish steps to get us there.

We all agreed that, for the first few months anyway, someone needed to take Jake outside every hour, until he grew accustomed to his new routine. Whenever he accomplished what we all longed for him to accomplish, we would shower him with verbal praise and tasty treats. The telltale signs of an impending accident were circulated so that disasters could be averted. As we developed effective strategies, each one inched us closer to our goal. And today I can honestly say that the issue of where Jake relieves himself never crosses my mind. That's how predictable dear Jake has become. What once was a dream is now a present reality, and we're better than we were before.

Clearly, with Jake, the future state was obvious, so little mental effort was required to envision a solution. But depending on the problem you're trying to solve, you may need more imagination, ingenuity, and plain old faith. I'm not suggesting that problems will be easy or quick to solve. Take the long view. Slow and steady wins every race. Be patient.

You may need to pull back for a season, to daydream, to ponder, to look, listen, or think.

Let me show you a more substantive example of what I mean.

Recently, another of my colleagues, Jeffrey, faced a dilemma of far greater consequence than our situation with Jake the dog. Jeffrey is a deep thinker with a quick wit, an expansive heart, and a hearty laugh. He's delightful to be around. As our director of coaching, Jeffrey is well-versed in all our problem-solving tools. This came in handy when a young man he knows (I'll call him Greg) encountered some problems. Jeffrey knew right where to start.

Greg had long dreamed of going to culinary school, so it was a big deal when, upon graduation from high school, he was accepted to ICC, the International Culinary Center in New York City. His parents coughed up tens of thousands of dollars for the young man to turn his dream into reality; but as we've seen, such destination-minded thinking often leaves us longing for more.

Greg arrived in New York and registered for classes, but he soon realized he had made a mistake. He missed the opportunity to take one class altogether and had to drop a second class because he hadn't taken the prerequisite yet. When his first-year schedule was found lacking by the school's administrators, they issued him his first "ding."

Soon thereafter, he was caught drinking in the dorm—his second ding.

What he didn't know but was about to find out the hard way was that at a highly selective school like ICC, it's two dings and you're out. Greg was expelled from the program of his dreams, and the fees he had paid were not refundable. He was furious. His parents were furious. Now what was he supposed to do?

Grudgingly, he packed up his dorm room, headed back to his parents' house, and got a job waiting tables. If he couldn't attend culinary school, at least he could do something in the food-service industry. Before long, however, living at home became too much to bear, and he decided to move out of his parents' house. He had recently started dating a young woman, and she agreed to let him move in with her.

Jeffrey said that this is where things really began to career downhill.

"Greg quit his job at the restaurant because he didn't think he was making enough money. But at least it was a job. At least it was a paycheck. He had nowhere else to go!"

He had been paying rent to his girlfriend, so when the paychecks stopped coming in, she kicked him out.

"Eventually, I had trouble reaching him," Jeffrey said, "and then I found out why. His girlfriend had bought his phone for him—and she kept it for herself when they broke up."

So now Greg had no culinary-school degree, no job, no place to live, and no phone. Things were not looking good.

It would have been easy for Jeffrey to leave this kid to find his own way; but knowing that so much of unlocking our own potential involves helping others unlock theirs (a topic we'll cover more fully in chapter 10), Jeffrey ran toward Greg instead of running away.

"His current state was obvious to both of us," Jeffrey said. "He was hanging out with the wrong crowd, blowing his time and money on stuff that could wreck his life, and

THINK OF THE POSSIBILITIES!

believing things about himself that were complete and utter lies. We both agreed on his current state.

"The future state? That was tougher to pin down. I could see a future for this kid that he couldn't yet see for himself. All he saw was further struggle, further disappointment, further hopelessness, further pain. But I knew he was talented. I knew he had gifts. I knew he could build a valuable life for himself. I knew he could win. As far as I was concerned, my role was to bring into view the future state that I knew for sure could be his."

Jeffrey began having weekly conversations with Greg (who, fortunately, had bought a new phone), during which he prompted the young man to articulate his desired future state.

"I simply kept asking questions," Jeffrey said, which by now you know I think is a pretty fantastic place to start.

Jeffrey would ask him, "The dynamics you're facing—are they what you hoped would be true of you at this stage in your life?"

Greg would moan and say, "No."

"What dynamics would you like to be true for you, then?"

Greg didn't have an immediate answer for that.

When new drama entered the equation, Jeffrey asked Greg, "How's that working for you?"

When Greg's friends would drag him away from becoming the man he said he wanted to be, Jeffrey would ask, "What types of friends do you want to attract, and what are the implications of that for the person you want to become?"

It took a long time, but eventually Greg went from borrowing Jeffrey's beliefs about his future to buying into those beliefs himself.

"We're still hard at work," Jeffrey recently told me. "And we will be for quite some time. But I'm convinced that as Greg and I keep speaking aloud his desired future state and he assumes the task of becoming the kind of person for whom that future state is a reality, he'll get there."

I believe Jeffrey is right. Regardless of what a person—any person—has or hasn't done, simply planting his or her feet on the path begins to unlock potential.

Allow me to give you one more example of the power of the current state/future state tool. We begin with one man, a deeply troubled neighborhood, and a beloved sport he hoped would save the day.

Part of our country's unfortunate history is that, for many decades, we enacted laws that prohibited ethnic minorities from living in certain areas. Real-estate maps were redlined, with boundaries fixed on the zip codes where African Americans and Latinos, for example, could purchase homes. In the 1920s, if you were a black woman or man living in Los Angeles, California's most populous city, the only place you would be approved for home purchase was either in Watts, an independent city south of downtown, or in the north part of South Central LA, the broader region of Los Angeles north and west of Watts.

Over the next twenty-five years, fueled in part by President Franklin Roosevelt's ban on racial discrimination in defense-industry and government hiring during World War II, a flood of minorities looking for weapons-manufacturing and ship-building jobs moved into the LA Basin, turning the South Central area into an overcrowded ghetto.

By 1940, the Ku Klux Klan had already infiltrated most of the country's urban centers, including Los Angeles. Minority gangs began to form to fight back against white intimidation. In 1965, with race tensions having reached fever pitch, a routine stop by a white police officer of a black man suspected of driving under the influence of alcohol sparked the infamous Watts riot, which lasted three full days and claimed thirty-four lives. Fearing for their safety, many of the few remaining whites in South Central fled, leaving a raw, angry, hurting community behind.

According to gang expert Alex Alonso, who is now a professor of Chicano and Latino studies at Cal State Long Beach, "The end of the 1960s was the last chapter of the political, social, and civil rights movement by black groups in LA, and a turning point away from the development of positive black identity in the city."[2]

Researchers with the National Gang Center note that "black Los Angeles youth searching for a new identity began to mobilize as street groups. This process also widened the base of black gangs into two camps, Crips and Bloods . . . particularly in the public housing projects."[3] The surge in gang activity all but ensured that "available positive role models were kept to a minimum and that the role models who were around belonged to the street."[4]

The increase in gang membership carved new lines of segregation in an already segregated area and led to an increase in gang violence. Then, in the early 1980s, came crack cocaine, which was like pouring gasoline on a raging fire. For those who were innocent bystanders to the trend, a quiet sense of desperation set in.

The scene was undeniably bleak. And yet hope was on its way.

In 1985, Oris Smiley—everyone calls him Dino—was approached by Alvin Willis, his longtime mentor.

"Dino," Willis said, "you're ready. I'm turning the Drew over to you."

"The Drew" was a six-team summer basketball league that Willis had started in 1973 to keep young boys off the streets of South Central LA during the months when school was not in session. Willis was a teacher at Charles Drew Junior High on Compton Avenue, and he noticed that misbehavior rose disproportionately during the summertime, when kids had too much idle time on their hands. He was impressed by the level of participation in those early years, but now it was time to take the league to a new level. He knew that Dino Smiley was the guy who could do it, given his shared passion for the community and its kids.

Up to that point, Dino had been the scorekeeper for the league. Most every weekend, he could be found perched atop a tall aluminum ladder in the middle school's gym, for hours at a time, keeping careful watch on the games in progress below.

Dino loved the Drew, and back when he was in eighth grade he'd seen a problem.

"We had guys, but no uniforms," he said with a laugh during an interview I did with him recently. "So I went to the local plumbing store and said, 'You should sponsor our boys' jerseys.' I must have sounded more confident than I felt, because they said okay. Two weeks later, every player had his own jersey, with Drew League printed proudly on the front."

Dino was still in his twenties when Mr. Willis handed things over to him, but he was up to the challenge. Shortly after he took over, the league grew from six teams to ten, and then from ten to sixteen, and from sixteen to twenty-eight, where it stands today, some forty-five years after its quiet start.

Year after year, May through August, guys would come together on the hardwood—five games on Saturday, five games on Sunday—and invest their energies in something more productive than defending their turf. As Dino recounted the evolution of the Drew League, I wanted to stand and cheer. Such *vision*. Such *passion*. Such *commitment*. This guy is absolutely the real deal.

"In the eighties, things were pretty rough," Dino said. "Corner boys were still battling it out with anyone from a rival gang who had the nerve to step onto their street. Our boys were getting shot—sometimes killed. Something had to change."

Mustering courage he wasn't sure he possessed, Dino went to the leaders of every nearby gang and begged them for a reprieve.

"Just on the weekends," he said, "while our guys are playing . . . can you stop with the killing, please?"

Astoundingly, the gang leaders said yes. Still today, for fifteen weeks every year, the corner of Compton and Fireside is a relatively safe place to be.

Over time, news about the Drew began to spread. Not only did local streetball notables want in on the action, but collegiate athletes and NBA stars began showing up as well.

A favorite memory of Dino's is the time he told Laker legend Kobe Bryant that he couldn't play.

It was 2011, during an NBA lockout, and Kobe was looking for some live play. He called Dino—which was easy for anyone to do, since the man published his personal cellphone number on the Drew's website—and said he wanted to come down for the championship game, the biggest game of the season for Drew participants.

Given Kobe Bryant's stature in professional basketball, you might assume that Dino told him, "Yes! Please! Come play!" But that's not what happened.

"We'd be pleased to have you, you know that," Dino told Kobe. "But no can do on the playing time. You know the rules. Gotta suit up at least once during the summertime to get minutes in the big game. Can't tilt the championship game, I'm afraid. But you come watch. You sit with me."

Kobe went, joining the ranks of such basketball luminaries as LeBron James, Kevin Durant, James Harden, Russell Westbrook, Baron Davis, J. R. Smith, Paul Pierce, Klay Thompson, Paul George, and countless other top players who have participated in the Drew League over the years.

I'm not at all a basketball person, but I am a *possibilities* person, and Dino Smiley embodies possibilities about as faithfully as anyone I've ever known.

"Carly, I didn't care what happened with the basketball games," Dino said. "I just wanted to keep our kids alive."[5]

The *possibility* that Dino envisioned? It was that the boys he regarded as surrogate sons would grow into responsible men someday. The summer league was simply a strategy. The objective was *life* and *peace* in his neighborhood.

Let me draw your attention to three key aspects of Dino's story that I believe can be implemented by anyone, anywhere—like *you*—who is impact-hungry today.

Whenever you find yourself squaring up against a problem you're determined to solve and yet you're tempted to lose heart—either because the issues seem so big, your ability to address them seems so small, or both—I hope you'll recall these three reminders, typified by Dino from the Drew League: *suspend judgment*, *speak truth*, and *seek hope*.

The landscape that Dino surveyed back in 1985 was a terribly grim scene. Yet Dino chose to preserve his buoyancy and keep his belief intact by refusing to focus on the negative. It would have been easy to write off the community and set up shop somewhere else, where life was quieter, easier, and saner—and who would have blamed him? Instead, Dino dug in. Although acknowledging that the situation was daunting, he believed it could change. He chose to see the possibilities instead of wallowing in the way things were. And I have to believe that his willingness to *suspend judgment* is at least part of what saw him through.

At the same time, Dino was anything but naive about the gravity of the situation. As he rallied other passionate people to help him expand the league that Mr. Willis had founded, they all understood how high the stakes were: Kids were dying left and right. He was realistic—clear-eyed, you might say—about the gang activity in the area. He was tuned in to the truth. But he didn't give that truth more power than it deserved; rather, he *spoke truth* and then forged ahead.

Finally, in Dino's story, I see the beautiful capacity to *keep seeking hope*. This is a trademark of optimism: When our current belief starts to waver, we borrow belief from a past success. All those years that Dino was sitting atop that ladder, keeping track of games and cheering guys on, he was racking up belief that the league was working, that a new culture was taking hold. When the going got tough—as it always does—and things became stressful, Dino had a decision to make: Would he hand over his power to fleeting circumstances, or would he *show up*, *step up*, and *lead*?

By now, you know how things panned out for him, and for the thousands of men whose lives he affected because he made the choice to stand strong. My question for you is this: Will you commit to doing the same?

Behavioral scientist Daniel Pink says that asking "Why?" can lead to understanding; but asking "Why not?" is what leads to breakthrough. This is the "suspending judgment" phase we looked at in Dino Smiley's story.

Why not safe space instead of a gang-infested neighborhood?

Why not a group of young men that the rest of the world has written off becoming world famous for their basketball league?

Asking "Why?" can lead to understanding; asking "Why not?" leads to breakthrough.

Asking "Why not?" will help you to suspend judgment while you address your current state and future state issues. Here are a few questions to help you balance realism and optimism. First, on the side of realism:

1. What really is the problem I'm facing?
2. Who else is affected by this problem?

3. What are the intricacies and nuances involved?
4. What have I learned from evaluating it from all perspectives?
5. What obstacles might keep us from flourishing?
6. What will delay us, deter us, or demoralize us along the way?

And then, on the optimism side of the equation:

1. What would make it better?
2. Who will be empowered, blessed, and positively affected if things are better?
3. What might that look and feel like?
4. What is needed to achieve this better state?
5. Who else can contribute and support us?
6. What will accelerate and sustain our progress and success?

I hope you'll take whatever time you need to think through this part of the journey, so that you and your fellow problem solvers aren't caught off guard later on. "Go slow to go fast," I often remind my coaching clients. Give yourself room to thoroughly assess reality on the front end and it will help keep a spirit of optimism alive as you work. Less reactivity equals more stamina to persevere. Being confident of the solution you're seeking increases the likelihood that it will be found.

Holocaust survivor Elie Wiesel once said, "Life is not a fist. Life is an open hand waiting for some other hand to enter it

. . . into friendship."[6] What a magnificent truth about perspective. And about engagement. And about hope. When you have witnessed and survived the largest genocide in history, it takes enormous courage and strength of will to choose optimism instead of pessimism.

Less reactivity equals more stamina to persevere

Right alongside the practice of seeing possibilities is the unflappable belief that no matter how rough the streets, no matter how loud the cries, no matter how deep the pain, no matter how dark the night, the power that resides inside you is greater than the power of the circumstances that threaten your joy.

part three

THE PROMISE OF THE PATH

chapter nine

NO GIMMES HERE

Promise No. 1:
Problems Will Get Solved

IN ALL THE YEARS I have been focusing my time, energy, and attention on problem solving and teaching others the nuances of problem solving, I have found only one group for whom the problem-solving tools—choosing path over plan; choosing courage, character, and collaboration; looking for creative possibilities—didn't work. That group is made up of people who don't *want* to solve problems. That's how it seems, anyway.

In the world of psychotherapy, this is nothing new. Some people, regardless of the severity of their problems, simply don't want to get well. And because they don't want health and wholeness for themselves, they don't have much interest in improving the world around them either. Maybe they just don't want to change. Other people want them to change— their spouse, their boss, their children, and their friends—but they themselves don't share that desire. At least not enough to do what it takes.

To be sure, solving problems that are big enough to warrant the attention of loved ones often requires something of a change of *identity*—from a smoker to nonsmoker, from addict to clean, from dropout to fully enrolled. Changes in identity, whether positive or negative, can be a terrifying prospect for some. I think of those slaves freed by President Lincoln's Emancipation Proclamation who stayed on the plantations where they had suffered years of abuse and grueling work because they couldn't imagine how they would survive as free women and men. Or of an abused spouse who stays with her abuser because she cannot envision life apart from him. Sometimes it seems better to remain in a situation we know, even as that reality squelches our soul.

Maybe people don't want to solve their problems because of plain old fear. Change requires an investment—of attention, of time, of energy, of strength. For some people, that investment seems way too big. They fear they don't have what it takes. Or that they will fail. Or that they'll have to give up more than they'll gain.

There's also the lure of "playmates, playgrounds, and playthings," as Alcoholics Anonymous famously calls the environmental tugs that make it tough to positively improve one's life. For example, if you're surrounded by self-focused people who aren't all that interested in having a positive impact on the world around them, it will be difficult to break away from that mind-set to forge a new path. Difficult, but not impossible.

Another reason that problem perceivers refuse to become problem solvers is that the pain simply isn't that bad. However, as writer Elizabeth Appell suggests, the day may come when the risk to remain tight in a bud becomes more painful than the risk it takes to blossom.[1]

I've been around my fair share of tight buds. Perhaps you have too. What a marvelous thing it is when at last they begin to unfurl.

There are people who know they have a problem, but for whatever reason will not take the first steps necessary to solve that problem. And there are people who think they are doing something positive, but who aren't willing to engage fully enough to make a real contribution to problem solving.

The very human tendency to avoid engaging in the art of problem solving now has a name: *slacktivism*. According to the *Oxford English Dictionary*, which added the term to its publications in 2016, slacktivism is "the practice of supporting a political or social cause by means such as social media or online petitions, characterized as involving very little effort or commitment." For those who are averse for one reason or another to actually solving problems, slacktivism—also known as *clicktivism* or *armchair activism*—must feel like a dream.

People pretend to be engaged in something important, something that *looks* like problem solving, even as they do nothing of substance or permanence to support the cause.

Lest you think I'm exaggerating, slacktivism has already been subjected to study. To wit, researchers at the University of British Columbia and Florida State University tested "the notion that slacktivist-style 'token displays of support' lead participants to engage in more costly and meaningful contributions to the cause."[2] They found that "those whose initial act of support is done privately (for example, writing to a member of Congress) are more likely to engage in deeper, more costly forms of engagement later on. Those whose initial support is public (i.e., through posting to Facebook or Twitter) are less likely to engage more deeply. Moreover, . . . most appeals for token engagement 'promote slacktivism among all but those highly connected to the cause.'"[3]

From 2012 to 2015, I chaired Good360, an Alexandria,

Virginia–based nonprofit that helps companies donate excess goods to charity instead of throwing them away. During my tenure, we pioneered a technology innovation that has since turned into a highly successful platform in the realm of disaster recovery. This solution was needed in real time, because only months before our launch, Superstorm Sandy, the deadliest hurricane of the 2012 season, came barreling up the Eastern Seaboard. The storm affected states from Florida to Maine, and as far west as Wisconsin. Streets were flooded, subway lines were cut, tunnels were rendered impassable, and countless homes were destroyed. The damage totaled nearly $70 billion before the storm headed back out to sea.

The American spirit being what it is, people across the nation quickly rallied to help. Lots of people. Images of the damage, captured by news cameras and cell phones alike, spread rapidly through social media; in response, generous men, women, and children headed to their local superstores to purchase blankets and diapers, children's clothing and socks, toothbrushes and hairbrushes, vast quantities of underwear, packages of ramen noodles, and countless other supplies, and promptly shipped those goods to New York and New Jersey, to the Carolinas and Georgia and Maine. There was just one small problem with all this well-intentioned aid: Those goods weren't the things that people needed just then. Or ever.

It takes, on average, three years for a community to recover from a major disaster. That means about 60 percent of what is donated in the first six weeks after a catastrophe is totally trashed. People can't use the things that are sent—either because there is no distribution system for getting the size-XXL undies to the size-XXL bums, or because underwear is the last thing on people's minds when they're trying to get back to what remains of their homes or find members of their families. As Sandy receded, the National Guard put out an all-points bulletin begging the kind and generous citizens of the United States to *please* quit sending stuff. I'll never forget the piles upon piles of "gifts" that were bulldozed right into the dump.

Motivation? Totally pure.

Execution? Left a little to be desired.

Our platform at Good360 allowed people in need to say, "Here is what we need this week." And also, "Please keep all the rest of your stuff." So, diapers arrived when diapers were needed. Blankets arrived when people were cold.

In 2014, First Lady Michelle Obama made headlines right before Mother's Day when she tweeted a picture of herself holding a handwritten sign that read, "#BringBackOurGirls." The girls she was referring to were the more than two hundred girls abducted from a school in Chibok, Nigeria, on April 14, 2014, by Boko Haram, a militant Islamic group in West Africa. In her public address to the nation, Mrs. Obama said, "What happened in Nigeria was not an isolated incident. It's a story we see every day as girls around the world risk their lives to pursue their ambitions."[4]

She confirmed that her husband—then-president Barack Obama—was doing everything he could do to support the Nigerian government's efforts to both find the missing girls and bring them home. "We can only imagine," she said, "the anguish their parents are feeling right now."[5]

Sobering, right? Of course it was. Anyone with half a heart felt compelled to do something to help. Or at least they feigned helpfulness. Celebrities such as Kim Kardashian, and many others, held up pieces of paper on which they had scrawled, "#BringBackOurGirls." Countless thousands of the not-so-famous also joined in, hashtagging their hearts out, retweeting demands for justice, offering "thoughts and prayers" to the families in pain.

There's nothing necessarily wrong with these demonstrations of support for those poor Nigerian schoolgirls. It's just that most people did little more than tweet their "involvement" and concern before they moved on. Worse yet, some pretended that they were part of the solution. And the girls? Four years after their kidnapping, some had been rescued, some had been freed, and some had reportedly been killed; and more than one hundred of the original group were still missing, still being held against their will.

Please don't misunderstand: I am not saying that nothing good comes from raising awareness by hopping on the bandwagon, hashtagging our support for causes, and pumping our fists and shouting, "Things must change!" I'm simply suggesting that if we want to see meaningful change, if we want to create substantive and lasting solutions to the very real problems we face, we must pay more than fleeting attention, we must invest more than anecdotal support, we must devote more than "hearts" and "favorites." We must *see, listen, learn,* and *work.* Anything less than committed, purposeful action will only earn us the title "Most Activity with Least Accomplishment."

When we are faithful to stay on the path to our fullest potential, problems will actually get solved. Often when I say these words, I get blank stares in response. Sometimes, the reason that problems aren't getting solved has less to do with fear or slacktivism and more to do with lack of know-how. Sometimes we just don't know where to start.

I have felt this way myself on more than one occasion when faced with huge, festering, and seemingly intractable problems. The issues are so big and so complicated that the natural first response is to feel completely overwhelmed. I soon learned that I needed a system, a paradigm, a tool to dissect and unravel problems; a way to cut massive problems down to more manageable, bite-sized chunks, so we could begin to digest them and make real progress toward solving them.

I call this tool the Leadership Framework. It addresses the *what*, the *who*, and the *when* of big change. The *how*, as you have probably surmised, centers on the qualities of courage, character, collaboration, and creatively seeing possibilities. And the *why?* That's the difference between the *current state* and the *future state*. We can *go* somewhere better than where we are now. We can *be* someone better than we are now. We can *do* better than the way things are now. In other words, we can—and we *must*—challenge the status quo so that we change the order of things for the better.

When trying to solve problems in an organization or group, we can become so overwhelmed by the complexity of what we're trying to do that we begin to shortchange or neglect certain things, or we focus only on the aspects of problem solving that we truly enjoy. These aren't necessarily conscious decisions; it's simply what happens when we're dazed and confused. The framework will lend predictability to the arduous tasks of problem solving and brokering changes. It reminds us to stay focused on every important aspect of the problem, not just the easy or fun parts. In other words, the framework gives us a complete picture of the work we must do to achieve our desired future state.

The Leadership Framework®

1. GOAL & STRATEGY
What problem are we solving?
What are we trying to accomplish?
What is our mission?
What is our desired outcome (goal)?

4. SHARED EXPECTATIONS
What's it like to be part of this effort?
What behaviors are encouraged/discouraged?
How does conflict get resolved?
What shared values bind us together?

2. SUPPORTING STEPS
Who is going to do what?
What don't we have that we need?
What procedures do we need to put in place
What will we prioritize to achieve our goal

3. TRACKING STEPS
Which results are truly meaningful?
How will we measure our results?
How will we know if we're making progress toward our goal?

As the name suggests, the Leadership Framework has four sides, like a frame.

The top side is reserved for step 1, the *goal* and the *strategy* to achieve that goal.

The right side is for step 2, the *supporting steps*: Who will do what? What procedures do we need to put in place?

The bottom side is step 3, the *tracking steps*: How do we measure our progress?

The left side is for step 4, *shared expectations*: How will we behave with each other?

Goal and strategy, supporting steps, tracking steps, and *shared expectations*—it's as simple and as complex as that. Let's look at each step in turn.

<hr />

Step 1 of the Leadership Framework is where you will answer the question "What is our goal?"

This is a *future-state* assessment, and as we saw in chapter 8, it is important to think critically about the future. What possibilities are you believing in, related to this problematic part of your life? What do you hope will transpire in coming days? What new reality do you hope to enjoy? For the woman in India who accepted the loan from Opportunity International, it was a better life for her and her family. For my friend and colleague Jeffrey, it was seeing Greg gainfully employed. For Dino Smiley, it was seeing the kids in his neighborhood make it to manhood in one piece.

What is the goal for you?

My team gives me a hard time for chronically trying to control my environment. Whenever I get into any of their cars, for example, I monkey with the AC. I adjust the car's seat position. I block the sun from my eyes. Whenever I check into a hotel, I spend a full twenty minutes nesting into my room. Every light on, suitcase unpacked, and clothes neatly put away. When I get home in the evening, I tend to putter around the house for half an hour, shutting cabinet doors that my husband opened, wiping off counters, clearing clutter, adjusting lights. I really, really like control.

But of course, even for so-called perfectionists and control freaks, many things are beyond our control. Most things, actually. But the one thing that is always within our realm of control is our choices. When working to define the problem you'll solve, start with what *can* be solved. Though perfection is never attainable, progress and improvement are within your grasp.

The first and most important question you must answer as you work to solve your problem is this: *What is my goal?* The rest of the framework is there to help you achieve progress and improvement toward that goal; in other words, changing the order of things for the better.

The reason it is so critical to declare a clear, unmistakable, and doable goal is that once you and your fellow problem solvers charge ahead in pursuit of change, something will go wrong. (The going always gets tough.) You will face an obstacle you didn't foresee; you will encounter criticism from naysayers; you will get the flu and lose problem-solving steam—whatever the case may be for you, you will be certain you're on the wrong path. You will be tempted to alter the goal to fit the awful reality you're experiencing now.

Listen to me: You are not on the wrong path! Do not change your goal! Pushback and setbacks are an inevitable part of the problem-solving process. Stay the course. Trust your preparation. Let your diligence pay dividends.

Step 2 of the Leadership Framework involves noting your supporting steps. In other words, what big-ticket things will you prioritize in order to achieve your goal? For Casey's dog, Jake, our supporting steps included (1) tasking someone with hourly walks; (2) heavily rewarding Jake with treats when he did his business outside; and (3) learning to spot the telltale signs that his bladder was about to explode.

For a group of disconnected neighborhood families who wanted to create *community*, their supporting steps included (1) rotating the hosting of monthly street-wide potlucks, (2) pulling together a team for their town's charity fun run that summer, and (3) inviting residents to post periodic updates on Facebook so that others could stay in touch with their goings-on.

For a small town reeling from a rash of teen suicides in the area, supporting steps included (1) scheduling monthly gatherings where teens, parents, and counselors could discuss what they were seeing and how they were feeling; (2) blitzing the area with the phone number of a suicide hotline, in case other teens were feeling distressed; (3) meeting with school board members who could relax the district's homework policy for a season, thereby reducing external stress; and (4) teaching families how to more wisely manage the calendar so that "quality time" could occur more often.

For an urban shelter struggling with a decrease in giving, their supporting steps centered on such initiatives as holding open-house events for people in the community to come see the shelter's services, and creatively telling the stories of people they'd helped, to build a vision for the future.

As you plot your own supporting steps, keep in mind that you may not be able to name all of them right away. Even so, I'll bet you can identify one or two to get you started. Between you and your problem-solving compatriots, my guess is you'll know more than you think you do. Here's a simple prompt: What do we not have today that we'll need—to either innovate, build, or acquire? Let your answer to that question drive your steps.

A word of caution: In groups of all kinds—formal and informal organizations and families alike—the tendency at this step is to want to use what I call the *nuclear option*. In professional settings, the nuclear option is often reorganization. Executives, especially, think that reorgs solve everything. But truth be told, they are very rarely the supporting steps needed to move forward on the path.

Reorganizations are sometimes necessary to ensure that the right people are doing the right work. Usually, however, reorgs create the illusion of progress while failing to solve the real problems. In fact, they're often just time-consuming and expensive activities that create a lot of new problems. Beware of *activity* that masquerades as problem-solving progress but turns out to be busywork.

In a personal context, the nuclear option often means assuming that the only way you can reach your goal—whatever that goal may be—is by taking drastic measures, such as divorcing your spouse, ditching your friends, or quitting your leadership role with the PTA. This simply is not the case. Remember, true collaboration requires that we approach problem solving with our three key phrases in mind: *I long to learn*, *I crave connection*, and *I refuse to go it alone*. Assume that the people closest to you are prospective partners in solving your problem, rather than saboteurs who are bent on tripping you up.

Step 3 of the Leadership Framework involves a thing called *tracking*: first deciding which results are truly meaningful, and then measuring the results you get.

What *can't* we track these days? We can track the steps we take, the calories we eat, the number of deep sleep cycles we enjoy each night, our heart rate, our pulse rate, our every financial transaction, whether we're getting optimal fuel efficiency in our car, and more. Clearly, tracking isn't a new idea for most people; the key is knowing what to track.

As it relates to problem solving, keep in mind that what you measure is what people will pay attention to. On the flip side, no one will care about the things you don't track. Simply stated, what gets measured is what gets done.

Beware of activity that masquerades as problem-solving progress but turns out to be busywork.

What will you measure toward your goal?

A sales manager I met who was having trouble hitting her quarterly quotas finally decided to invest fifty bucks in an automatic dialer that tracked the calls she made. She simply used available technology to merge her online database with the dialer and then hit *Start* as she held the phone. The dialer recorded how many numbers were dialed in a given hour, how many clients picked up the call, how long

What you measure is what people will pay attention to. No one will care about the things you don't track.

each call lasted, how many voice mails were left, and so forth. Not surprisingly, she blew the next quarter out.

A group of women came around a mutual friend who was on the brink of divorce. The friend had a scheduled vacation coming up, and the group agreed to work through a twelve-chapter self-help book during the weeks leading up to her departure. They decided at the outset which twelve dates they would meet. By declaring the dates ahead of time, they were able to see who would be absent during which weeks and come up with a plan for virtually enfolding those group members. Their metric was to take attendance at each of the meetings where they discussed the twelve chapters.

I know of a group of pastors in a western state who banded together to see that every child in their area's foster-care program was adopted into a loving "forever family" from one of their congregations and given the resources they needed to thrive. Tracking that total from seven hundred kids in need to five hundred to less than two hundred today has been wildly motivating for them.

We pay attention to what we measure. This is true 100 percent of the time.

Now, what can you do if one of your supporting steps isn't measurable in a straightforward way? Let's say that you and four acquaintances have decided to volunteer at a local community college that is holding classes to teach immigrants how to navigate American life. The five of you care equally about the work, yet you and one of the others can't seem to get along. You're a planner; she's more spontaneous. You need things laid out; she waits to see what unfolds. You make decisions quickly; she likes to linger with her thoughts for a while. On and on the differences go. My point is that it's better to acknowledge your differences as soon as you detect tension, rather than pretending the issue doesn't matter—that it's "no big deal."

One of your supporting steps might be centered on empathy—learning to esteem each other's perspectives and to value the contribution each person makes. This might include practicing the questions we looked at in chapter 7; or reading a book on empathy together and discussing the key themes; or pulling another group member into occasional discussions about how to allow for differences among friends. Still, how do you measure progress for something as nebulous as "relational healing"? How do you measure progress on "how well we're getting along"?

My advice is to create a rating system that is easy for everyone to use. In the example above, you and your colleague might decide that, for one or two months, you'll take a minute or two at the end of the week to *score* how the two of you did. Your rating system might be a one-to-five scale, from *poor* to *excellent*, for example. Following a planning session with your team during which you felt that familiar frustration about your colleague's lack of planning, you might honestly say, "I give us a two this week. I still don't see things from your perspective. I feel annoyed and put out instead."

Sensing your frustration, she'll probably agree.

Over time, as intention and real effort begin to transform your relationship, that score will likely rise. You'll start to notice that because of your colleague's fluidity, your team is able to respond to needs more quickly than if you were encumbered by too many layers of process. Your colleague may be able to see that because of your attention to detail the people you're serving are better served. At some point, if you're like the scores of once-disgruntled associates I've been around, you'll both be rating your interactions with *fives* so frequently that you'll put the practice to rest.

Whether related to weight, money, satisfaction, or any of a million other categories, numbers do not lie. True, they cannot tell the entire story of progress made, but they surely shed meaningful light.

Step 4 of the Leadership Framework looks at expectations—that is, the *culture* of your group. What's it like to be part of this joint effort? What behaviors are encouraged? How does conflict get resolved? What are the shared values that bind you together? Where are the boundary lines? What constitutes a *foul*?

In my experience, people don't listen to what you *say* as much as they watch what you *do*. So, you have to *walk it out*. Likewise, people don't respond to what you say you believe as much as they respond to how you actually live out your beliefs.

Talking through the expectations that will mark your experience is a useful, level-setting step. This part of the process honors not only the achievement of the goal you're pursuing, but also the *means* to that worthy end.

Don't shortchange this step. In many organizations or teams, *culture* or *shared expectations*—or, more accurately, "What is it really like to work here?"—is often referred to as the "soft stuff." Metrics? Hard stuff. Who's in charge of doing what? Hard stuff. Strategy to achieve our goals? Definitely hard stuff. Consequently, most organizations and teams will downplay working on culture and discount the importance of actually walking the walk instead of just talking the talk. (Remember Glen the Lawyer?) They think all that "soft stuff" is for the human resources department, not for the rest of us.

In truth, the soft stuff is the hardest stuff of all. I refer to it as the *software* of any team. And as we all know from our many devices, if the software is messed up even a little, everything gets messed up. (How often have you had to download a new software update?)

How people *work* together makes all the difference in how much they will *achieve* together.

Here's an example. One of the very positive things that flowed from the values behind the HP Way was something called the open-door policy. On all the offices around HP, either there were no doors at all, or the doors were always open. The emphasis was on transparency and teamwork. Of course, there are times when privacy is required and a door must be closed. But open doors are far better for collaboration.

How people work together makes all the difference in how much they will achieve together.

Think about it. A closed door literally shuts people out. If someone is walking down the hall with an idea and they come to a closed door, how many times will they hesitate or turn around because they're not sure if it's worth the interruption? What gets lost in that hesitation?

And here's the other thing: How much time do people spend speculating about what's going on behind those closed doors? When people don't know what's going on, they tend to imagine the worst—never the best. That's why transparency is so important. When a door is closed, people start to won-der, *Who's in there? Why? What are they talking about? Maybe they're talking about me! Or something that will negatively affect me.* Secrets, whether trivial or explosive, have power precisely because they are closed up and locked away. Open the door.

———

Recently, I took a client through the construction of a Leadership Framework. After we had mapped out the group's overarching goal, the supporting steps they'd need to take, the tracking mechanisms they would use to measure their results, and the expectations that would guide them, one of the staff members sat back in his chair and said, "Gang, we can't go back."

His statement was both a caution and an invitation. For the first time, perhaps, he was seeing—really seeing—the possibilities for where he and his colleagues could go, and he desperately wanted that future state for them. He didn't want to return to "the way things used to be." Once we move forward, we can't go back. The past needs to stay in the past.

But the invitation in his words was compelling. Once the group had clarified where they were headed, and why; how they would get there, and when; what would be rewarded, and in what ways, they were determined to stay the course. There was a sense of shared responsibility tethering them one to another; they were resolved to blossom and thrive.

As you go through similar paces, my guess is that you and those you've linked arms with will feel the very same way. Ennobled. Empowered. Accountable. Valued. Ready. Eager. Resolved.

chapter ten

TO-THE-BRIM LIVING

Promise No. 2:
Potential Will Be Unleashed

WHEN I GET ON the elevator on the first floor of the corner bank building in Old Town Alexandria and ride to the third floor, where the Unlocking Potential offices are located, I always have the same feeling. I am grateful and happy. I'm grateful for our team, for our work, and for our partners. I'm happy that I'm able to spend my time as I do. Sure, I have bad days just like everyone else, but most days are filled with gratitude and happiness.

Recently, on the heels of a Leadership Lab, I sat for an interview about our foundation's work.

"So, these principles you espouse," the interviewer said, "what benefit can a person expect to realize who follows your methods faithfully, over time?"

I sat with the question for a moment before answering.

"Less fear, more joy," I replied.

The more I practice what I've been preaching through-out these chapters, the less fear I have. Granted, I've been working on building courage for quite some time now; but as I told you before, we never fully get over our fears. We can learn to quiet them, we can learn to subdue them, we can learn to relegate them to a place on the back shelf. But at some level, fear will always be with us. It will always rear its head. So when I told the interviewer, "Less fear," what I meant was less of being *mastered* by fear. As I've learned to run *toward* problems instead of running away from them, and as I keep trying to always choose the best version of myself over all other forms, fear has had far less sway over my decision-making. It occupies less and less of my brain.

Likewise, following the winding path instead of adhering to a plan ushers in something I recognize as joy.

If you've spent any time around the fields of physics or engineering, you're familiar with the concept of *sine*. A sine wave is a continuous up-and-down curve, generally depicted as rising above and below a horizontal axis. Now picture those peaks and valleys as emotions—the highest of highs and lowest of lows, followed by another high, another low, another high—and you have a decent understanding of what is celebrated in our culture these days. Society by and large has fallen prey to the magnification and amplification of *circumstances*. More specifically, to our collective *reactions* to those circumstances. This makes sense, I suppose: If everything is truly either an all-time-greatest experience or a tragic, epic fail, it stands to reason we'll respond by being really up or really down.

But I've found it's all a sham. In truth, there are very few actual *crises* and very few *best-ever* experiences. Consequently, so much of the energy we expend is a colossal waste.

Multiple studies on the effect of interruptions on our ability to focus on a task have shown it takes the average person at least thirty minutes—and in some cases, an hour or more—to regain their pre-interruption concentration, once the distraction has come and gone.

How about we choose to disembark from the societal roller coaster we've willingly put ourselves on? You and I both would agree that it's impossible to avoid all distractions in life—and who would want to, anyway? If we care about people, we must accept that they are unpredictable and very rarely operate on our time frame. But since when does it make sense to ride the "sines of our times," expending so much energy going up and down?

I bring this up because I've noticed that, as I practice following the path, there is a steadiness, a sureness, in my step. No longer do I feel subjected to the wild swings of cultural enthusiasm.

We're outraged! We're elated! We're fuming! We're rejoicing! We're incredulous! We're euphoric! We're irate!

Increasingly, I feel like the horizontal axis on the sine-wave diagram, steadily and efficiently cutting its way through all the ups and downs. And though there was a time in my life when I would have said that this kind of evenness sounded terribly boring to me, thankfully that time has passed. These days, I find that letting go of the unending anxiety on one side and the unbounded hysteria on the other has become a wonderfully welcome part of my life.

When I was living life on the campaign trail in 2015 and early 2016, I was often asked by folks in the media what it was like to be "a woman CEO"—and later, "a woman presidential candidate." My answer was not entirely facetious: "I don't know," I replied. "I've never been a man."

In the same way that I will never know anything but being a woman, I believe I will never know anything besides trying to always operate at full potential—ideas flying, cylinders firing, heart engaged. And my commitment to you is this: If you will devote yourself to the practices we've talked about—the perspective, the courage, the character, the whole bit—you too will never know anything but maximized potential. If you will choose to live this way, I can all but guarantee that a day will come when you will wonder, *When's the last time I wasn't content?*

My four "really cans" for you are these:

1. You really can learn to view problems as opportunities.
2. You really can choose the practices that will help you thrive.
3. You really can live from your fullest potential.
4. You really can help others do the same.

You really can learn to view problems as opportunities.

This idea that problems are the pavement under our feet, the very thing that tells us we're on the right path, is not just lip service for me. It's how I live my life. Solving problems is what we were made for, remember?

We see beauty and are moved to capture it.

We see need and are moved to meet it.

We see suffering and are moved to eradicate it.

We see hope and are moved to multiply it.

We see love and are moved to return it.

We see joy and are moved to relish it.

We see pain and are moved to alleviate it.

We see peril and are moved to avoid it.

We see grace and are moved to reflect it.

Yes, we get tired and frustrated. Yes, we can be harsh with our words. Yes, distractions still tempt us. Yes, we think our way is best. But at the core of who we are, we're focused on making things better. We're determined to learn, to change, to grow. That's why certain problems make your heart beat faster, make you long to jump into the fray. You were made for solving those problems. You have the needed resources to solve those problems. You owe it to yourself and others to play through.

When you encounter such problems, then, my advice to you is not to wallow, but to get to work.

A few examples, if I may:

If seeing the teachers at your child's school being under-valued and underpaid drives you nuts, rally a work group of like-minded warriors and get busy blessing teachers' lives.

If seeing a bullying boss at work makes those tiny hairs on your neck stand up straight, gather a group of like-minded warriors and overcome evil with good.

If seeing undeveloped land on one corner and people who are homeless and hungry on the other corner makes your brain want to explode, gather a group of like-minded war-riors to plant a garden, get people fed, change some lives.

In other words, be encouraged by seeing the *potential*, not the peril, of such problems.

In a recent World Economic Forum article, author Martin Burt said it well:

Social innovation and social entrepreneurship is about creating new paradigms and new ways of addressing old social problems. Social innovation has to do with impact, and it has to do with scale. These are new ways of seeing problems as opportunities, of seeing how to look at the same problem from a different perspective, and bringing light to a solution

that may be right there under our nose[s]. . . .
What social entrepreneurs are doing [is] bringing a
flashlight to the room.[1]

This type of seeing requires some training on our part,
Burt says. We must decide to see the possibilities. We must
decide to think future state. "We need to look at problems
not as something that is impossible to address, but as something that we can accomplish. . . . Every single social problem
is an opportunity."[2]

Yes, yes, yes, yes, yes.

So if you detect rampant job dissatisfaction in your
department, do you see a problem, or do you see potential?

If you detect loneliness in your neighborhood community, do you see a problem, or do you see potential?

If you detect apathy among your friend group, do you see
a problem, or do you see potential?

If you detect a sharp, judgmental spirit in your extended
family, do you see a problem, or do you see potential?

When we start to see that we were made to solve problems, and that our deepest sense of fulfillment rises only
when we're accomplishing that task, we will relish the arrival
of new problems. We will celebrate; we're on the right path.

I'm confident you will feel that same sense of elation I
feel upon getting to work each day. You're right where you're
supposed to be, doing precisely what you're meant to do. You
are seen, and you are supported. You are flanked by those
who care. You have a perspective that is worth hearing. You
need not strain or hustle or strive. You can be amazing. You
are prepared for the problems you face.

—

When we start to see that we were made to solve problems, we will relish the arrival of new problems.

—

You really can choose the practices that will help you thrive.

If you've been giving away your power for a while, this truth may take some time to sink in; but I promise you it's true. We all choose who we want to become. I encourage you to start today choosing the practices that will help you thrive.

Today you will become more fearful or more courageous. The choice is yours.

Today you will become more scattered or more integrated. The choice is yours.

Today you will become more uncooperative with others or more cooperative. The choice is yours.

Today you will become more of a pessimist or more of an optimist. The choice is yours.

You will expand your knowledge, or not.

You will increase your circle, or not.

You will act from compassion, or not.

You will wait patiently for life, or not.

You will challenge your own prejudices, or not.

You will practice gratitude, or not.

You will help others, or not.

You will let others speak first, or not.

You will ask for help, or not.

You will encourage others, or not.

These and a thousand other choices are *yours*, without exception.

You really can live from your fullest potential.

This may come as a surprise to you, but the most common reason for not operating at peak capacity is a three-letter word: y-o-u. I'm talking to myself here as well, which is why I can tell you with full confidence that if something's in your way, most likely it's you.

You're the one who frets.

You're the one who fusses.

You're the one who allows fear to have its way in your mind.

You hesitate. You equivocate. You overanalyze. You sit. You stew. You play "just one more round" of Candy Crush (or whatever your weakness is), while the solutions at hand go untapped.

I met Nikki following a client event and knew immediately she was the real deal. Tie-dyed shirt and baggy pants, Rastafarian hairdo that was graying at the temples, colorful socks with ultra-flat tennis shoes, not an inch over five feet tall—you couldn't have missed her if you tried.

The most common reason for not operating at peak capacity is a three-letter word: y-o-u.

"Carly," she said, "that's some no-nonsense teaching of yours. Right up my alley. Get 'er done, right?"

Nikki laughed her great laugh, as her smile stretched far and wide. In the conversation that followed, I learned about the most recent solutions Nikki had provided to her workplace.

"I keep track, for days that don't pan out so well," she said. "Gotta keep the faith—am I right?"

The more I talked with Nikki, the more I wanted whatever she had. Wise, witty, joyful, astute—this woman had it going on.

We parted company about twenty minutes later, but her

words rang in my ears all night long. This was a woman who had chosen the path, who had opted for peace, contentment, and joy. She'd refused to be thrown off by life's ebbs and flows; instead she allowed steadiness to be her guide. As a result of her faithfulness, her team had netted some huge results.

Does Nikki get it right every time, every day? I think you know the answer to that. But she is exactly where she is meant to be, doing exactly what she's meant to do. And she knows it. She's solving the problems she finds all around her, lifting people up as she goes.

I know the current struggles we face are serious—I do. I know they can weigh us down like a ton of bricks. I know the days can feel long and hope can be fleeting. And yet I also know this to be true: We can still make a positive contribution, day by day. We can still affect things for good. We can still emanate joy. We can still rise above our circumstances. We can still be fulfilled and live fulfilled, and then turn and show others the way. Yes, we really can.

You really can help others do the same.

In May 2008, a friend of mine, then–secretary of state Condoleezza Rice, asked me to create an empowerment fund for women in countries where they are most oppressed. We both recognized the vast opportunities she and I have been given in America, and we were compelled to be good stewards of the lessons we had learned and the resources we had acquired along the way.

Condi grew up in the segregated South, the only child of a teacher and a preacher. We each had found our way through diligent effort and a bit of luck. After all, we came of age at a time when this country was finding its conscience regarding the treatment of women; she and I were grateful for that favored spot.

More immediately, though, we were compelled by a truly tragic turn of events.

Two days after Christmas in 2007, the first woman ever to head a democratic government in a Muslim-majority nation, Benazir Bhutto of Pakistan, was assassinated. She had served as prime minister twice—from 1988 to 1990 and again from 1993 to 1996. Though many viewed her as a controversial figure, she was extremely instrumental in championing democracy and women's rights in that part of the world.

On the day of her death, Ms. Bhutto had been campaigning ahead of her country's January elections. Following a political rally in Rawalpindi, Pakistan, shots were fired at her and her associates. By six o'clock that evening, she had died. We were determined not to let her death be in vain.

We lost no time gathering groups of employees of the US Agency for International Development (USAID) and the US Department of State for discussion. What bubbled to the surface was a mutual desire for justice, opportunity, and leadership on behalf of women around the world. We began mapping out strategies fairly quickly: vocational training, microlending, awareness-building regarding women's basic rights worldwide, and how to advocate for the liberty they deserved—many of the same things Benazir Bhutto had stood for. How we hoped she would have been proud.

There were lots of great organizations doing good work. I believed many of the best were local, focused on their communities, but they were also so small they weren't getting the attention and the funding they needed. So we decided to lift them up.

On the administrative side, we decided to make this a joint effort, bringing together ten partners from the private sector and both the State Department and USAID from the public sector. In terms of the recipients of the grants we would issue, organizations would simply submit applications that detailed the thrust of their cause.

Shortly after Condi and I confirmed the details of our plan, she delivered a formal statement in Washington, DC:

> In an age where women are climbing to new heights, we must pause for a moment and direct our concerns toward those who have been left behind. . . .
>
> Across this globe, we see signs of women standing up for freedom, standing up for justice and demanding opportunity. And I am proud of the work the United States is doing to support them. I am equally proud of our corporate partners for their initiative to empower, educate, and inspire women across the globe. We know that it is only by working together that we can ultimately effect change for women around the world.[3]

As is always the case, things took longer to move ahead than we hoped, and for the first full year following our official announcement, we gave away not a single dollar. But we did raise our first round of funding, and at last grants were ready to be made. I beamed when I saw the headline on an advance release from USAID's office in early June 2009: "'One Woman Initiative' Announces First Grants to Women's Organizations in Five Nations."

The article began,

> The One Woman Initiative, a one-year-old public/private initiative to empower women in countries with significant Muslim populations, today announced its first grants, totaling more than $500,000 to five grassroots organizations in Azerbaijan, Egypt, India, Pakistan, and the Philippines. The OWI grants are being made to locally focused organizations with results-oriented programs providing women access to legal rights, political participation, and economic development.[4]

I lingered over the details of those first five grants, imagining in my mind's eye the good they would do. When one woman—just one woman—is empowered, the world benefits. When that woman is granted access to information and training, to resources and opportunities, to advocacy and freedom and care, she can raise up her entire family, and on occasion, her community at large. To embolden ten women or one hundred women or one thousand women—as these first five grants would do—wasn't a matter of addition but of exponential effect. When entire swaths of the population in various villages and regions are given access to broad-based support, and when they are invited to participate in local workplaces, and when they are allowed to offer their expertise, opinions, and strength—well, in that scenario, the ensuing effect can be huge.

―――――――

As you think of all you've read in this book, and as you reflect on your own life and your opportunities for impact, perhaps you feel small and inadequate just as often as you feel powerful and strong. Whenever you feel small, think of a pebble tossed into a still pond. The tiny pebble enters the water with barely a splash, but from there it sends ripples far and wide. Seemingly inconsequential agents can catalyze significant change. If just one person discovers that he or she has power; if just one person is shown his or her vast gifts; if just one person is taught how to stand firm and speak; if just one person learns how to dream, then ripples will begin to move across the world.

Whenever you feel small, think of a pebble tossed into a still pond. The tiny pebble sends ripples far and wide.

Knowing is not enough; we must apply.
Willing is not enough; we must do.
JOHANN WOLFGANG VON GOETHE

ACKNOWLEDGMENTS

A book, like any other worthwhile endeavor, is a team effort. I was blessed to have a great team alongside me every step of the way at Tyndale House Publishers, with people who believed in this project from the beginning.

Likewise, everyone at the Unlocking Potential Foundation provided both inspiration and hard work. Whenever I get stuck, I think of them and the work they do.

My husband, Frank, as always, was a constant source of encouragement and wise counsel. Our granddaughters, Kara and Morgan, gave me someone to talk to in my mind when the words did not flow easily onto the page.

And three other special acknowledgments:

To Ashley Wiersma: Thank you for truly understanding the purpose of the words on these pages.

To Casey Enders: Thank you for your passionate commitment to bringing these ideas to life.

To Frank Sadler: Thank you for your steadfast loyalty and determination to see this through.

NOTES

MOMENT OF REVELATION

1. Mary Oliver, "The Summer Day," in *House of Light* (Boston: Beacon, 1990), 60.

CHAPTER 2: THE TRAGEDY OF THE TERMITE

1. Gertrude Stein, *Everybody's Autobiography* (1937) (New York: Cooper Square, 1971), 289.
2. "Tom Brady—There Has to Be More Than This," interview with Steve Kroft, *60 Minutes*, November 6, 2005, video, 1:07–1:31, www.youtube .com/watch?v=4HeLYQaZQW0.

CHAPTER 3: WHAT'S WRONG IS ALSO WHAT'S RIGHT

1. Kobi Yamada, *What Do You Do with a Problem?* (Seattle: Compendium, 2016), n.p.
2. Ibid.
3. Katie Muse, "Alabama 4-Year-Old Using Allowance to Feed the Homeless," Fox 4, April 13, 2018, www.fox4news.com/news/u-s-world/alabama-4-year -old-using-allowance-to-feed-the-homeless.
4. Mary Todd Lincoln, letter to Mercy Ann Levering, June 1841. Cited in Justin G. Turner and Linda Levitt Turner, *Mary Todd Lincoln: Her Life and Letters* (New York: Alfred A. Knopf, 1972), 25.
5. See a discussion about the origins of this aphorism in "Whether You Believe You Can Do a Thing or Not, You Are Right," Quote Investigator, February 3, 2015. https://quoteinvestigator.com/2015/02/03/you-can /#return-note-10545-1.

CHAPTER 4: DECISIONS, DECISIONS

1. David Richo, *The Five Things We Cannot Change: And the Happiness We Find by Embracing Them* (Boston: Shambhala, 2005), xi.
2. Interview with Gary Zukav in Oprah Winfrey, *The Wisdom of Sundays: Life-Changing Insights from Super Soul Conversations* (New York: Flatiron Books, 2017), 48.
3. Shawn Achor, "The Happy Secret to Better Work," TED video from TEDxBloomington, May 2011, 7:48: www.ted.com/talks/shawn_achor _the_happy_secret_to_better_work?language=en#t-458474.
4. DeVon Franklin with Tim Vandehey, *Produced by Faith: Enjoy Real Success without Losing Your True Self* (Nashville: Howard, 2012), 12. Italics in the original.
5. "Who We Are," Girl Scouts of the United States of America, https://www.girlscouts.org/en/about-girl-scouts/who-we-are.html.

CHAPTER 5: WHAT ARE YOU AFRAID OF?

1. Paul Solotaroff, "Trump Seriously: On the Trail with the GOP's Tough Guy," *Rolling Stone*, September 9, 2015, www.rollingstone.com/politics /politics-news/trump-seriously-on-the-trail-with-the-gops-tough-guy -41447/. Italics and punctuation in the original.
2. Transcript of GOP Presidential Debate, aired September 16, 2015, CNN.com, www.cnn.com/TRANSCRIPTS/1509/16/se.02.html.
3. Mark Twain, *Pudd'nhead Wilson* (Mineola, NY: Dover Publications, 1999), 60.
4. Daniela Schiller, "Snakes in the MRI Machine: A Study of Courage," *Scientific American*, July 20, 2010, www.scientificamerican.com/article /snakes-in-the-mri-machine.
5. See Matthew 16:26.
6. Rebecca Ray, *Be Happy: 35 Powerful Methods for Personal Growth & Well-Being* (New York: Rock Point, 2018), n.p.
7. Scott Cacciola and Christine Hauser, "One After Another, Athletes Face Larry Nassar and Recount Sexual Abuse," *New York Times*, January 19, 2018, www.nytimes.com/2018/01/19/sports/larry-nassar-women.html.
8. Ibid.

CHAPTER 6: WHO YOU ARE WHEN NO ONE'S LOOKING

1. John S. McCain, "John McCain, Prisoner of War: A First-Person Account," *US News and World Report*, January 8, 2008 (originally published May 14, 1973), www.usnews.com/news/articles/2008/01/28/john-mccain-prisoner -of-war-a-first-person-account.
2. "The HP Way," Hewlett-Packard Alumni Association website, updated September 11, 2017, www.hpalumni.org/hp_way.htm.
3. Susan David, "The Gift and Power of Emotional Courage," speech at

TEDWomen 2017, New Orleans, LA, November 2017, 9:24–10:38, www.ted.com/talks/susan_david_the_gift_and_power_of_emotional _courage/transcript?language=en.

4. David Brooks, *The Road to Character* (New York: Random House, 2015), 10–11.

5. Jim Rohn, *7 Strategies for Wealth and Happiness* (New York: Three Rivers Press, 1996), 53–54.

CHAPTER 7: BECOMING A BETTER *US*

1. "Global Apple iPhone Sales from 3rd Quarter 2007 to 3rd Quarter 2018 (in Million Units)," Statista, www.statista.com/statistics/263401/global -apple-iphone-sales-since-3rd-quarter-2007.

2. Ibid. See also, "Unit Sales of the Apple iPhone Worldwide from 2007 to 2017 (in Millions)," Statista, www.statista.com/statistics/276306/global -apple-iphone-sales-since-fiscal-year-2007.

3. Joshua Rothman, "A New Theory of Distraction," *New Yorker*, June 16, 2015, www.newyorker.com/culture/cultural-comment/a-new-theory -of-distraction.

4. "Technology Addiction 101," addiction.com, www.addiction.com /addiction-a-to-z/technology-addiction/technology-addiction-101.

5. Adapted from "Technology Addiction 101."

6. Phil Jackson, interview with Oprah Winfrey, *Super Soul Sunday*, June 16, 2013. See also "Phil Jackson Tells Oprah Why Basketball Is A 'Spiritual' Game,'" *Huffington Post*, June 14, 2013, www.huffingtonpost.com /2013/06/14/phil-jackson-oprah-basketball-spiritual_n_3435221.html.

7. Dr. Henry Cloud, quoted in Dan Schawbel, "Dr. Henry Cloud: How to Manage Boundaries in the Workplace," *Forbes*, May 10, 2013, www.forbes .com/sites/danschawbel/2013/05/10/dr-henry-cloud-how-to-manage -boundaries-in-the-workplace/#1cdd90af681d.

8. Adam Grant, "The Problem with All-Stars," *WorkLife with Adam Grant* podcast, ted.com, www.ted.com/talks/worklife_with_adam_grant_the _team_of_humble_stars/up-next#t-71540, 1:11.

9. "On Stage Interview with Wade, Bosh and James—July 9, 2010," NBA. com, www.nba.com/heat/news/on_stage_interview_wade_bosh _james_2010_07_10.html.

10. Michael Lewis, "The No-Stats All-Star," *New York Times Magazine*, February 13, 2009, www.nytimes.com/2009/02/15/magazine /15Battier-t.html.

11. Ibid.

12. Grant, "The Problem with All-Stars," 6:12–6:39.

13. Proverbs 16:18. See also Luke 14:7-11.

14. Brené Brown, "The Power of Vulnerability," RSA Events, July 4, 2013, www.youtube.com/user/theRSAorg/search?query=power+of+vulnerability.

CHAPTER 8: THINK OF THE POSSIBILITIES!

1. Colin L. Powell, *My American Journey* (New York: Ballantine Books, 1995), 613.
2. Alejandro A. Alonso, "Racialized Identities and the Formation of Black Gangs in Los Angeles," *Urban Geography* 25, no. 7 (2004), 668.
3. James C. Howell and John P. Moore, "History of Street Gangs in the United States," *National Gang Center Bulletin*, no. 4, May 2010, 11–12.
4. James Diego Vigil, *A Rainbow of Gangs: Street Cultures in the Mega-City* (Austin: University of Texas Press, 2002), 77.
5. Oris "Dino" Smiley, interview with the author.
6. Elie Wiesel, interview with Oprah Winfrey in "Oprah and Elie Wiesel: Living with an Open Heart," *Super Soul Sunday*, December 9, 2012, http://static.oprah.com/pdf/201212-sss-elie-wiesel-transcript-v4.pdf.

CHAPTER 9: NO GIMMES HERE

1. The quote "And the day came when the risk to remain tight in a bud [was] more painful than the risk it took to blossom" is widely attributed to Anaïs Nin, but it does not appear in any of her known works. In 2013, Elizabeth Appell, former director of public relations for John F. Kennedy University in Orinda, California, claimed to have coined the phrase in 1979 for a brochure she created for the university. See "Who Wrote 'Risk'? Is the Mystery Solved?", the *Anais Nin Blog*, March 5, 2013, http://anaisninblog.skybluepress.com/2013/03/who-wrote-risk-is-the-mystery-solved.
2. Laura Seay, "Does Slacktivism Work?" *Washington Post*, March 12, 2014, www.washingtonpost.com/news/monkey-cage/wp/2014/03/12/does-slacktivism-work/?utm_term=.2879883a9e38. See also Kirk Kristofferson, Katherine White, and John Peloza, "The Nature of Slacktivism: How the Social Observability of an Initial Act of Token Support Affects Subsequent Prosocial Action," *Journal of Consumer Research* 40, no. 6 (April 2014), 1149–66, www.jstor.org/stable/10.1086/674137?seq=1#page_scan_tab_contents.
3. Seay, "Does Slacktivism Work?"
4. "Michelle Obama 'Outraged' over Nigeria Kidnapped Girls," *Reuters*, May 10, 2014, https://af.reuters.com/article/topNews/idAFKBN0DQ09P20140510.
5. Ibid.

CHAPTER 10: TO-THE-BRIM LIVING

1. Martin Burt, "Social Entrepreneurs Seeing Problems as Opportunities," World Economic Forum, December 18, 2015, www.weforum.org/agenda/2015/12/social-entrepreneurs-seeing-problems-as-opportunities.
2. Ibid.

3. Condoleezza Rice, "Remarks at the 'One Woman Initiative' Fund for Women's Empowerment," May 12, 2008, US Department of State Archive, https://2001-2009.state.gov/secretary/rm/2008/05/104629.htm.

4. "'One Woman Initiative' Announces First Grants to Women's Organizations in Five Nations," USAID press release, June 3, 2009, www.usaid.gov/content/one-woman-initiative-announces-first-grants -womens-organizations-five-nations.

ABOUT THE AUTHOR

CARLY FIORINA is founder and chairman of the Unlocking Potential Foundation and Carly Fiorina Enterprises, organizations that invest in human potential by supporting leaders who are solving problems in their communities and places of work—equipping them with the behaviors, characteristics, disciplines, and tools they need to increase their leadership and problem-solving capacities.

Carly is a true leader and a seasoned problem-solver. She is a passionate, articulate advocate for problem solving, innovation, and effective leadership. Her mission is to inspire, equip, and connect individuals and teams to seize opportunities, face challenges, and accelerate impact.

Carly started out as a secretary for a small real-estate business and eventually became the first woman ever to lead a Fortune 50 company. In 1999, during the worst technology recession in twenty-five years, she was recruited to lead Hewlett-Packard. As she refocused the company on innovation and market leadership, revenues grew, innovation tripled, growth quadrupled, and HP grew to become the eleventh largest company in the United States.

Since leaving HP, Carly has focused her efforts on giving back to society. Prior to Unlocking Potential, she served as chairman of Good360, the world's largest product philanthropy organization, and as chairman of Opportunity International, a Christian-based organization that lifts millions out of poverty around the globe through microfinance. In 2008, she founded the One Woman Initiative in partnership with then–secretary of state Condoleezza Rice, to engage and empower women in Azerbaijan, Pakistan, Egypt, India, and the Philippines through increased access to economic opportunity.

In addition to *Find Your Way*, Carly has authored *Rising to the Challenge* and the *New York Times* bestseller *Tough Choices*.

Carly and her husband, Frank, live in northern Virginia near their daughter, son-in-law, and two granddaughters.